AF344564

The Sound of Silence

American University Studies

Series IV
English Language and Literature

Vol. 189

PETER LANG
New York • Washington, D.C./Baltimore • Boston • Bern
Frankfurt am Main • Berlin • Brussels • Vienna • Canterbury

Anju Kanwar

The Sound of Silence

PETER LANG
New York • Washington, D.C./Baltimore • Boston • Bern
Frankfurt am Main • Berlin • Brussels • Vienna • Canterbury

Library of Congress Cataloging-in-Publication Data

Kanwar, Anju.
The sound of silence / Anju Kanwar.
p. cm. — (American university studies. IV,
English language and literature; v. 189)
Includes bibliographical references and index.
1. Lawrence, D. H. (David Herbert), 1885–1930—Characters—Single women. 2. Women and literature—England—History—20th century. 3. Single women in literature. 4. Silence in literature. 5. Speech in literature. 6. Short story. I. Title. II. Series: American university studies. Series IV, English language and literature; vol. 189.
PR6023.A93Z6363 823'.912—dc20 96-41218
ISBN 0-8204-3660-7
ISSN 0741-0700

Die Deutsche Bibliothek-CIP-Einheitsaufnahme

Kanwar, Anju:
The sound of silence / Anju Kanwar.
–New York; Washington, D.C./Baltimore; Boston; Bern; Frankfurt am Main; Berlin; Brussels; Vienna; Canterbury: Lang.
(American university studies: Ser. 4, English language and literature; Vol. 189)
ISBN 0-8204-3660-7
NE: American university studies / 04

The paper in this book meets the guidelines for permanence and durability of the Committee on Production Guidelines for Book Longevity of the Council of Library Resources.

Printed in the United States of America

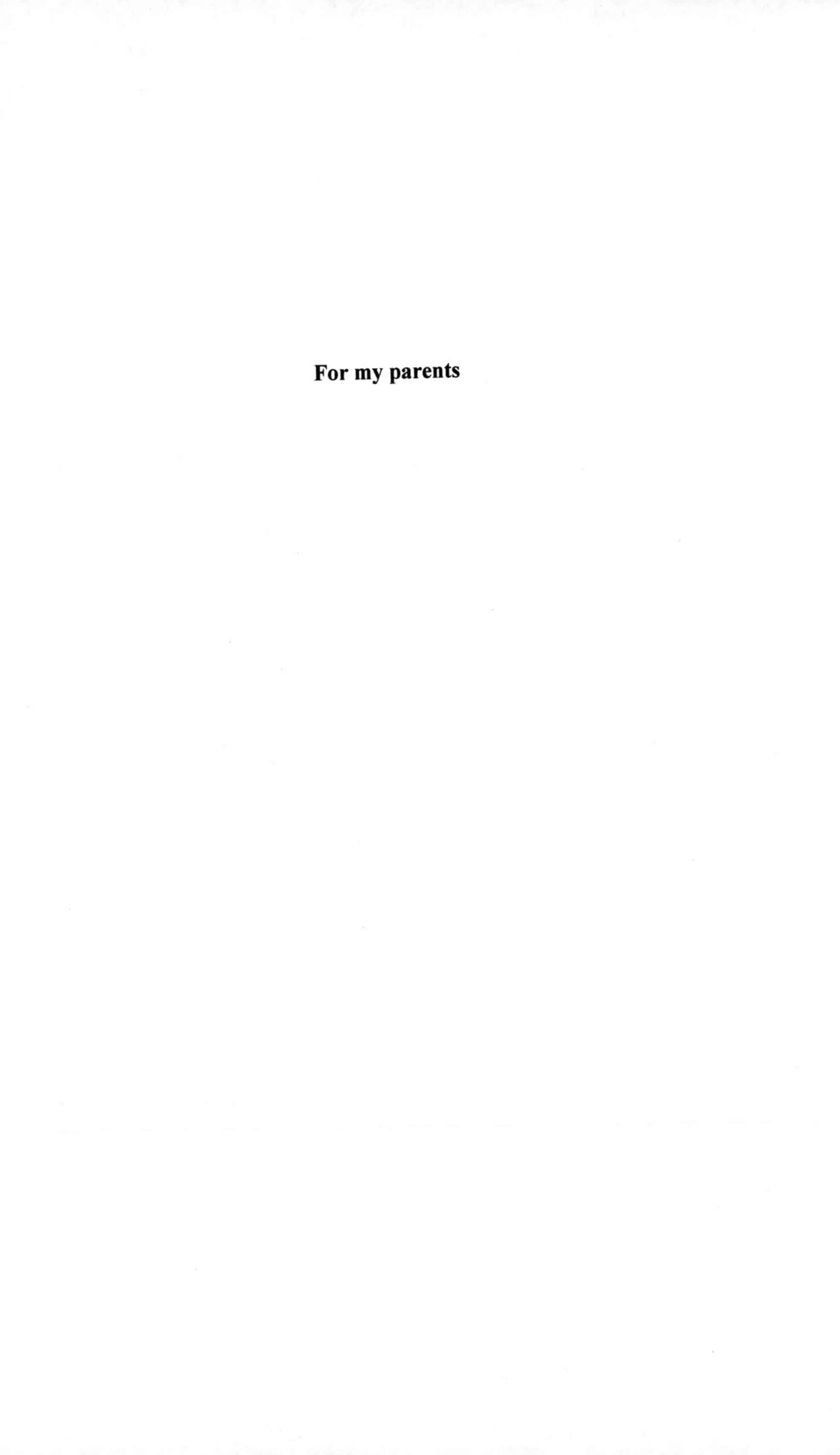

For my parents

Acknowledgments

Since this book began as a doctoral dissertation, in many ways I owe thanks to all the people who helped me get there. Most especially, Professors James Mellard and Mary Sue Schriber, Northern Illinois University, who helped me find my voice and give it expression.

To the editors and other editorial staff at Peter Lang Publishing, Inc., I owe thanks for their invaluable suggestions, patience with and understanding of the vagaries of my often shy Muse, as well as prompt and ready responses to my concerns at all times that helped me bring my project to fruition.

To Laurence Pollinger Ltd. and the Estate of the late Mrs. Frieda Lawrence Ravagli, I owe thanks for permission to quote from the letters of D. H. Lawrence.

To my friends, especially, Roshini George, Siu Chow, Andrea Manning, and Barb Owczarek, I owe thanks for their spoken and unspoken support. And for just being there.

To my parents, Lachhman Dass and Updesh Kaur, I owe the knowledge that courage is destiny.

Contents

Chapter 1

Introduction

Imaginatively [woman] is of the highest importance; practically she is completely insignificant. She pervades poetry from cover to cover; she is all but absent from history.

Virginia Woolf

I

Despite the fact that D. H. Lawrence often claimed he supported the feminist cause, feminist critics question his claims. On the one hand, as the self-proclaimed prophet of the woman's cause, Lawrence boasted that he would "do a novel about Love Triumphant one day" and that his "work for women [was] better [for them] than the suffrage" (quoted in Ross 14). Moreover, his portrayal of women characters—such as Hermione Roddice, and Ursula and Gudrun Brangwen in *Women in Love*, who are granted greater autonomy of speech than are many of their previous fictional counterparts—allows him to claim support of the feminist cause. Indeed, in the past, some feminist critics (for example, Dix in *D. H. Lawrence and Women* [1980]) have viewed his claims and works as evidence of his support for the woman's cause. On the other hand, some have castigated him for being staunchly anti-feminist: that, for example, is the judgement of Simone de Beauvoir in *The Second Sex* (1952), Kate Millett in *Sexual Politics* (1970), and Margaret Storch in *Sons and Adversaries: Women in William Blake and Lawrence* (1990).

One of the primary reasons that the battle between the feminists and Lawrence has continued since the nineteen fifties is that he frequently emphasizes essentialism in women. For example, in his essay "Do Women Change?" Lawrence says not only that "[h]umanity seems to have an infinite capacity for remaining the same" (539), but also—and worse—that "women don't change" (541). He asserts that women only evolve, that is, they go through phases where the same essence takes on different shapes through time. As a consequence, Lawrence views woman's history as an evolution from the position of the slave to one of independent self-assertion, at which point woman isolates herself. Independent, though isolated, the new woman achieves "modernity." Lawrence believes, however, that this "modernity" in women indicates the end of civilization and parallels the end of civilizations in the past because "modernity," independent self-assertion, violates and distorts woman's essence, what "woman" must be in the fundamental, natural ordering of things. While Lawrence asks us to learn from the past, he believes that the only way to avoid the end of our civilization is for women to be less assertive and return to an ordinary heterosexual way of life within patriarchy.

Lawrence discusses the evolving roles of women and men in history in another essay as well. In "Cocksure Women and Hensure Men," he complains that modernity in women has led to their appropriation of traditionally male roles and positions in society; in other words, women have appropriated the role of the "cock" or rooster as opposed to their "natural" role of hen. Since he believes that this modern position in women is unnatural, he asserts not only that has it led to undermining the men but also that it has led to the isolation of women from men and from themselves, and the reduction of their happiness. For example, Lawrence asserts that just as the men in his day are "timid, tremulous, rather soft and submissive . . . [,] the women step forth with a good loud *cock-a-doodle-do*!" (554). Here, Lawrence discusses "the tragedy of the modern woman" wherein, "[f]rightened of her own henny self, she rushes to mad lengths about votes, or welfare, or sports, or business" (555). By such means, Lawrence asserts, the modern woman outmans the man. "But, alas," he says, women's attempt to appropriate traditionally male roles "is all fundamentally disconnected" (555). In this essay, Lawrence posits woman's "cocksureness" not only as unnatural but also as unfruitful. He declares that since this new cocky quality in women is not natural but born out of fear of the hen in themselves, their essential and true nature, it is more pronounced in them than it ever was in men. Consequently, it leads to their isolation not only from men, but from their own essential selves. Lawrence thus believes that the isolation of the sexes from one another, together with the self-division within a woman, and what he regards as the end of civilization are a direct result of the more assertive and independent "modern" woman.

In "Matriarchy" (1928), Lawrence again ponders the "mystery" of woman.[1] He explains the effect of the new woman on the new man. He believes that just as the new "cocksure" women are products of fear of male supremacy, so in turn men, afraid of the new woman, find that fear is a reason for further asserting themselves. In this essay he suggests how men need not fear women's rule and how matriarchy need not be a system that devours the male. Rather, he discusses the benefits to men of a return to the matriarchal system of social organization. He believes that by returning to this social system men shall be totally free of social responsibility—from questions about inheritance and government—to pursue their own interests (549-52). Neglecting to focus on how women could grow within matriarchy, in this essay Lawrence focuses on viewing it as a social system that should not evoke fear in males but allow them to grow.

Lawrence's ideas, stressing the relation of women to men and the changing role of the new woman, have shaped literary reaction to Lawrence, that shape being further solidified by connotations of such a word as "cock." An apriori notion of Lawrence as anti-feminist and hence his fiction as one to be contested is the result. From John Bull's attack on *Lady Chatterley's Lover* to those of Kate Millett, Charles Rossman, and others, many studies focus either on the movement of the female characters toward marriage or on an analysis of a marriage relation or on the changing effect of women on men. A close look at these studies reveals their truncated pattern. Very few studies focus on the unmarried women characters in themselves. Rather, they are used as analytical handmaidens to probe the real interest of the criticism, the male characters. Androgyny, I believe, reigns in the critics as in Lawrence's fiction. Studies that do focus on them in Lawrence do so only to reconstruct the male characters; such, for example, is Declan Kiberd's focus in *Men and Feminism in Modern Literature*. Further, critics who focus on the psyches of female characters in Lawrence do so only to study how they affect the psyches of male characters and operate within the parameters of a traditional male-female relation; most of the earlier critics, such as Middleton Murry, would fit this category. By studying male and female characters as adversaries fighting for supremacy, critics primarily present female characters in Lawrence's works as though the only way to "see" them is through their relations to men.[2] Though these critical perspectives may be the result of the critics' own imposition of meaning or the result of their understanding of Lawrence's narrative presentation of women characters framed in the philosophy expressed in Lawrence's aforementioned essays, they all fail to recognize the significance of the unmarried female characters in themselves and by themselves. Only when coupled are they attended to. Their importance derives from the male, in Lawrence and in criticism of Lawrence.

Similarly, Lawrence's insistent focus on the heterosexual relation has contributed substantially to the derivative status that unmarried women have come to occupy in Lawrencean criticism. Critics such as Michael Black note that Lawrence speaks often of his belief in the heterosexual. He identifies war between the sexes as the real cause for all the troubles (such as war and the death of civilization) in the world: "I think the real tragedy is in the inner war which is waged between people who love each other" (quoted in Black 257). Lawrence believes that just as a degenerating heterosexual relation can cause the death of our civilization, so can our dying civilization be revived by its restoration: "I'll do my life-work," he says, "sticking up for the love between man and woman" (quoted in Black 257). Lawrence's letter to Arthur McLeod on 23 April 1913 expresses this belief in the redemptive power of the heterosexual relation: "I am so sure that only through a readjustment between men and women, and a making free and healthy of the sex, will she [England] get out of her present atrophy . . . I . . . write because I want folk—English folk—to alter, and have more sense" (quoted in Black 257). Because of his belief in the redemptive power of the heterosexual relation, Lawrence mystifies this relation. For instance, in a letter to Gordon Campbell in 1914, he says: "I believe there is no getting of a vision . . . before we get our sex right: before we get our souls fertilized by the female. . . . Because life tends to take two streams, male and female, . . . only some female influence . . . can fertilize the soul of man to vision or being" (*Collected Letters* I 291). He thus equates a healthy heterosexual relation not only with the restoration of civilization, but also—in the tradition of the Romantics—with the gaining of revelational vision.

Perhaps as a consequence of Lawrence's expressed belief in the all-pervasive power of the heterosexual relation, no study of Lawrence focuses exclusively on unmarried women functioning within women's history. But a steady development of feminist literary theory and criticism, and a new interest in culture, has opened up the study of writers such as Lawrence by recognizing new sub-groups and sub-cultures within the larger category of gender. As a gender category, unmarried women constitute one such group. My study makes visible a hitherto invisible group of Lawrence characters, female characters who have never married. Not only have the unmarried women characters often been ignored by critics of Lawrence, but at other times the lives and choices of these unmarried women have also been obscured or marginalized by androcentric readings of the texts. This has occurred despite the fact that his unmarried female characters cover a wide spectrum.

Indeed, Lawrence's unmarried women characters, characters who may have had relationships with both sexes, or none, but have not entered into the institution of marriage, range from the bold and sassy tram conductor Annie in "Tickets, Please," to the lesbian March in *The Fox*, and to the mythical androgyne, the man who died (Christ) and rose to seek out the woman of Isis in *The Escaped Cock* (in "The Overtone," Lawrence equates Christ with the female principle).[3] They also range in age. Most—such as Winifred in "The Witch a la Mode" and Emmie in "You Touched Me"—are in their late twenties or early thirties. But a few I discuss in my study—such as Miss Stokes in "Monkey Nuts" and Elaine in "The Primrose Path"—are in their late teens or early twenties and serve as counterpoints to their older counterparts. (I discuss the representations of each group in the short stories separately solely for the purpose of convenience.) They range across social classes as well. For example, while Annie in "Tickets, Please" comes from the working-class, Emma in "The Christening" and Aunt Cissie in *The Virgin and the Gipsy* come from the more genteel though impoverished middle-class, and Flora in *St. Mawr* comes from the upper-class. Together, these women show Lawrence's incorporation, for his fictional purposes, of age and class distinctions into his characterization of unmarried females in order to examine the relationship of these to the independent action of unmarried females.

In the past, if critics have studied unmarried female characters, they have done so to focus on them as examples of women who oppose male authority (through their independent behavior) and are "punished" with singleness.[4] As opposed to these critics, I focus on Lawrence's experiments in the portrayal of independence of these characters to demonstrate that Lawrence is much less fixed and far more exploratory in his presentation of them in the short novels than he is in the short stories. But Lawrence more than demonstrates their independence; he often portrays this independence—such as in "The Primrose Path" and "Tickets, Please"—as achieved by undesirable means or as undesired by the female. It moves, that is, *against* women's presumed essence and is therefore a failure. At the same time, even though Lawrence often demonstrates the failure of the female characters' attempt to be independent, his *depiction* defeats itself, exposing the insidious ways in which the patriarchy undermines the females and perpetuates itself. It proves to be patriarchy rather than a mystic womanly essence that accounts for the failure of these characters. Thus, his fiction reveals the underlying weakness of the patriarchy rather than of the new and independent woman.

As unmarried female characters have been marginalized by critics and in Lawrence's fiction, so Lawrence's short fiction has been marginalized as well, further contributing to limited readings of unmarried females. While many critics have studied his portrayal of women characters in the longer fiction and poetry, the development of feminist insights into Lawrence is blocked by a failure to examine fully the short as well as the long fiction. Even those critics who devote a chapter or two to Lawrence's shorter fictions often emphasize the novellas; because they sometimes include novellas under the same category as the stories, these studies also proceed at the expense of the short fiction, which is ignored for other reasons as well. Janice Harris suggests some reasons for the neglect of Lawrence's short fiction. For example, she suggests that the stories have escaped critical interest because of their sheer volume, swelled by the several different versions of these narratives. Another reason may be that the highly repetitive nature of themes within these stories suggests that they may be considered as mere training ground for Lawrence's later and major works (ix-xiv). But whatever the reason for the neglect, I believe that the short fiction remains a rich field to be explored—not least because it is in the short fiction that most of his unmarried women appear.

To date, there are only two published full-length studies of the short fiction: Kingsley Widmer's *The Art of Perversity: D. H. Lawrence's Shorter Fictions* (1962) and Janice Hubbard Harris's *The Short Fiction of D. H. Lawrence* (1984).[5] Both Harris and Widmer explore the short fiction in thematic terms.

Harris approaches women in Lawrence's shorter fiction in relation to Lawrence's growth as an artist. Her approach is a departure from Widmer's more thematic approach that divides the narratives into "clusters of perversity, ranging from tales that explore the attraction of the destructive woman to those that celebrate the death throes standing at the extreme of eros" (Harris x). While Widmer's focus is often unbalanced (he dismisses an alarming number of tales in a line or two), Harris carefully reconstructs the background of each tale and evinces a brief concern with feminist issues among several other concerns. But she sacrifices depth for breadth. Moreover, neither she nor Widmer focuses on unmarried female characters in the short fiction.

***

The neglect of Lawrence's short fiction and the unmarried female characters within it may be related, as well, to a move, in feminist critical practice, away from male-authored to female-authored works.[6] Some may wonder, in fact, why a feminist critic at the turn of the twentieth-century undertakes any study at all of D. H. Lawrence. I, however, join Sandra Gilbert in her assertion that though it is imperative to attend to the contributions of women,

> feminist criticism cannot limit itself to literature by women, for every text can be seen as determined by aesthetic and political assumptions about gender that might be called "sexual politics." Its fullest ambitions are to explore and decode all the hidden connections between "textuality and sexuality, genre and gender, psychosexual identity and cultural authority." (quoted in Showalter *NFC* 10-11)

Adrienne Munich, too, argues for continued attention to male-authored works. She believes that "[l]iterary texts linked by common inheritance and cultural recognition have been shaped by both men and women." Hence, she adds, "[r]evisionary interpretations which explore female influence in male-authored works are a vital enterprise for feminist criticism" (240). Munich acknowledges the feminist attempt to validate the traits assigned to the female through gynocentric readings, but asserts that by "polarizing literary criticism into gynocentric and androcentric criticism . . . [,] Showalter replicates the social categories of gender" (241). Munich thus suggests that "[i]nstead of viewing the criticism of male-authored texts as a mere act of interpreting works by the 'other,' feminist criticism can consider the active role of women in their production—how this two-sexed culture has produced gendered polarities which inform all its writings" (244). This shift in feminist literary approach as more "radically transformative . . . [in] impact" was recognized by Showalter herself in her later introduction to *Speaking of Gender*. Here, she admits that "talking about gender means talking about both men and women" (2). I align myself with Showalter, Gilbert, and Munich. By studying Lawrence's works, I insist that there is room for and value in feminist studies of both female-authored and male-authored works. Moreover, I believe that gender is a category of literary analysis, not merely of the literary analysis of female-authored works. Just as the critical community wouldn't limit archetypal or Lacanian reading to but one gender, feminists must be careful not to diminish their own work by reducing its scope.

***

Because previous studies on Lawrence's women characters marginalize unmarried women and because the popularity of Lawrence's longer fiction and poetry have obscured the value of his shorter works where the unmarried women occur most frequently, I am chiefly interested in studying the representations of unmarried women in Lawrence's short fiction, reading "feminist," reading against the grain. My study emphasizes the need to turn the spotlight from the female-threatened male, the married woman, and the woman tending toward marriage to the woman who remains outside the framework of relations governed by the heterosexual social contract, and outside the relations in which Lawrence himself, the Father and Law and Authority, may want the reader to be most invested. I shall argue for the recognition of Lawrence's unmarried female characters as an independent sub-group within the larger category of gender. By rejecting what Toril Moi calls "the prevailing image of the reader/critic as passive/feminine recipient of *author*itarian discourse" (25), I situate myself among feminists who recognize the need "to undo the patriarchal strategy that makes 'femininity' intrinsic to biological femaleness, and at the same time insist on defending women precisely *as* women" (82).

In my study, therefore, pledging allegiance to my precursors such as Kate Millett, who, explains Toril Moi, question the authority of the author/text to "expose the underlying premises of a work," I insist on the value of reading Lawrence's texts "against the grain" (24-25). My feminist reading of Lawrence's fiction, though "unfaithful" to Lawrence, the representative of the Father and Law, and even "unfaithful" to the fathers of criticism, expresses my *difference* from them. In the words of Jane Gallop, I adopt infidelity as a feminist practice. Reading "against the grain," for instance, I note that because Winifred Varley's withdrawal from a mouth kiss, in "The Witch a la Mode," is often viewed as a withdrawal from sex, she is equated with a witch. Significant to our understanding of this story and Winifred therefore is our understanding of the patriarchal associations with the term "witch" and our redefinition of it in feminist terms. Coutts's feelings of frustration at the moment of her withdrawal color his opinion of Winifred and have, in turn, colored androcentric readings of this text. But there is more than one (male) way of reading Winifred's withdrawal, for though she withdraws from the mouth kiss, she does not withdraw from Coutts's embrace. In fact, Winifred exercises her ability to act independently—by embracing her womanhood and taking charge. Thus, it is important for us to consider that it is *Coutts's* sexual frustration at her withdrawal that leads him to believe her behavior is unnatural. It is, moreover, his own fear of attraction to her that leads him to see her as a projection of inner desires of his own from which he needs to escape.

II

For the critic to tell the story of the unmarried female characters in Lawrence's short fiction, it is essential first to situate their story within that of actual culture. But how do we include their story within culture without changing history completely? What we *find* in such sub-groups is the group's history—one that the author may not have *intended* to write, but wrote nonetheless. The concealed is revealed, the margin is centered, the invisible woman is made *visible* by the feminist critic. In my study, I discuss the cultural history that forms the context from which Lawrence's female characters emerge. I do this to demonstrate the crucial relation between their treatment in culture in the past and their presentation in Lawrence's fiction. Moreover, I undertake another feminist task:

the pursuit of feminist criticism in the interests of social change. Where possible I discuss the impact of today's changing trends in the perception of this difference in culture that allow us to reassess Lawrence's presentation of unmarried females in relation to our present cultural reality, that we might better understand that reality and shape ourselves and culture accordingly. As I show the relation between past and present, I will often do the work of the historian. Edward Hallett Carr discusses the relation between the past and the present in his study of history. He defines history as a constant interaction, "a dialogue between the historian in the present and the facts of the past" (42). He sees the function of history as dual. First, it enables us to comprehend the society of the past. Second, it enables us to empower ourselves over society in the present (69). When we adopt Carr's assertions about the study of history for literary purposes, we realize that the relation of an individual (in this case the unmarried woman) to history places her in relation to a cultural tradition. This relation is a necessary prerequisite in the construction of *her* self, for all individuals are composites of their past and present. Further, a resolution with the past (both personal and cultural) is often essential for us to have any future.

We can more fully understand the Lawrencean text by situating it in the cultural and ideological and gender history in which it was created and on which it drew. Like most modern studies of domestic patriarchy, my reconstruction of that history looks back to the seventeenth century, when both the church and the state allowed women very little freedom and value. The term "patriarchy," as Margaret Ezell defines it, is "any social environment that is perceived as hostile to independent activities of women in spheres other than traditional domestic, nurturing roles" (3). Women who deviated from these patriachal norms often had to face public humiliation and physical tortures and were burnt as witches. But reconstructions of the history of women recognize the conflict between abstract ideas about women (masculine ideas) and women in the real world; "woman" versus real women. In reconstructing women's history, we realize—with Virginia Woolf—that although "Imaginatively [woman] is of the highest importance; practically she is completely insignificant. She pervades poetry from cover to cover; she is all but absent from history" (43).

Among feminists who have reconstructed women's history, Monique Wittig and Carolyn Heilbrun note the absence of women from history. The absence of women in history is especially apparent in our language, where the male typically represents the universal and where often the speech of women is silenced. Lawrence's texts accentuate the absence of women from history when his unmarried female characters are shown to be constructed—to borrow Lacanian terminology—by (a) male Other/others. Patriarchy as it were makes them mute. Critics add to this process of muting through inattention to these characters, who are thus rendered mute a second time. Feminists, however, pay attention to women's speech, even when uttered softly in the margin of the text. Indeed, the male imposition of silence on women's speech has provoked several studies on the nature of women's speech.[7]

Among others, Shirley and Edwin Ardener have made invaluable pioneering studies on the process of muting in women. In "The Representation of Women in Academic Models," Shirley Ardener asserts that women have largely been represented as the invisible and muted group in society. Where women have been visible, they have yet been presented as passive and silent objects. She suggests that this muting may be the result of either unconscious or deliberate choice by those who least wish to discriminate against women (3-5). Cheris Kramarae explains how muting can be the result of these two choices. She believes that since members of a culture do not equally contribute to the formulation of its language, the language therefore does not serve all its members equally (1). Further, since women are a subordinate group, they are made "inarticulate" by the dominant group in society (1). Kramarae, with Barrie Thorne and Nancy Henley, also explains another aspect of the problem of muting: because of the sexist construction of language, interruption and inattention to women's speech also contributes to women's silence: "[W]omen may be stereotyped as talkative because they are *expected* to be more silent . . . and in mixed-sex conversations women *are* more silent, with men tending to take more and longer turns to talk" (17). The three scholars agree with the poet Adrienne Rich that silence "is a presence/ it has a history/ a form/ Do not confuse it with any kind of absence" (quoted in Thorne, Kramarae, & Henley 17). Since much of women's history is imbedded in its silences, they assert that it can be re-constructed only by a re-appropriation and re-valuation of women's speech (17).

Even where women have been granted speech, they are still subordinated by patriarchal descriptions of the nature of it, as Lawrence does and as this study will deconstruct. According to Heilbrun, among other feminists, women's speech often lacks authority because of the ways it is characterized. Along with Mary Ellman, Heilbrun points out that when women are accused of "shrillness" and "stridency," the accusations often serve to exclude them from the power structure (11-25). Other terms serve the same purpose. Kramarae deplores how women speakers are labelled as "*shrews, bitches, cats, hens; shrill, sharp-tongued, and gossipy*" (xiii), and thereby stripped of effective power. Such labels, and others—as Julia Stanley's study of 220 terms used to describe women as sexual creatures—lead Kramarae to assert that sexual terms are demeaning to women and place them in "opposition to men" (xiii). She explains that women's opposition to men is also evident in the advice they are given on how to talk. Kramarae discusses how today this advice does not differ much from advice that was given to them in the Middle Ages. Her study, therefore, demonstrates that so long as women's speech continues to be undervalued, there is need for concern over the differences in male and female speech.

III

My reconstructive and evaluative study of the speech and silences of unmarried female characters in Lawrence's short fiction is based on the premise that figurative language such as metaphor and metonymy act as signifiers of Lawrence's unconscious values. Lawrence's tropes suggest two things. First, they demonstrate how he often perpetuates received cultural images (or ideas) of unmarried women in the interests of his art. Second, they demonstrate his narrative attitude toward the unmarried women. Let me discuss these claims in turn.

First, Lawrence perpetuates cultural stereotypes of unmarried women in his figurative language. Often this figurative language presents women in binary ways, as either madonna or whore, witch or angel, virgin or prostitute. In "The Witch a la Mode," for instance, Lawrence conjures old Puritan associations between seductiveness and attractiveness in a woman with witch-like qualities that disempower and destroy the male. In this story, when Bernard Coutts, while engaged to another woman, is unable to contain his attraction for Winifred Varley, his old love, he suggests by his figurative language that he can not control himself because she behaves like a witch. It is she at fault. Lawrence also perpetuates cultural stereotypes of unmarried women in "The Christening." In this story, Lawrence invokes the Biblical story of Christ's birth, but in his figurative language associates the single mother with both the madonna and the whore. In both these stories, Lawrence's tropes imbed his image of unmarried women. Using deconstruction as a tool to understand Lawrence's binary presentation of women, I argue that such presentations in culture and literature result from cultural and literary attempts to define the feminine in relation to the masculine—and to preserve and sustain the masculine by keeping alive the feminine, the binary opposition, on which the masculine depends for its existence and meaning.

My study of Lawrence's presentation of the unmarried women in relation to their cultural past in the short fiction reveals a persistent pattern. For instance, Lawrence often presents the younger and older unmarried females in the short stories and the short novels in similar ways: not only does he not explore their intellectual lives, but he primarily presents them in circumstances of defeat.[8] But Lawrence does differentiate between the older and younger unmarried women on the basis of their sexuality and speech. My study shows that while Lawrence often presents the young unmarried women as outspoken and assertive in action, he often presents their older counterparts as silent, chattering, or mad.[9] He also denies the older unmarried women (most of whom are in their late twenties and early thirties; one is in her forties) a sexual existence and a voice and presents them in the stereotypical and patriarchal terms of previous centuries. Further, Lawrence uses class distinctions to differentiate among the younger unmarried women. He demonstrates that younger unmarried women (such as Flora, in *St. Mawr*) who belong to the upper class do not so totally define themselves in relation to a male "other" as will younger unmarried women (such as Annie, in "Tickets, Please") who belong to the working class. Lawrence thus suggests that economic independence often precedes the unmarried woman's rebellion against gender definition by the patriarchy.

Second, like Lawrence's figures, the assertions and silences of his narrators on the subject of women suggest Lawrence's narrative attitude toward unmarried women characters. Assertions are easy to identify, but how do we identify silences in a prose text? Peter J. Rabinowitz offers us a methodology. In his article "Assertions and Assumptions: Fictional Patterns and the External World," he says that in a literary text assertions and silences about the issue under discussion help us to determine the relation between fiction and reality. The whole question of determining "reality," says Rabinowitz, can be understood by tracing the difference between the authorial and narrative audience. While there are some areas of overlap between the two audiences, he identifies the authorial audience as "assumed" and the narrative audience as "asserted." Rabinowitz explains how assertions often operate merely on the narrative level; while they are devices of characterization and tell the reader something about the fictive characters who utter them, they do not necessarily tell us anything about the author. Further,

> even if an assertion is intended as a "true" statement about the "real" world, and not simply about the author's imaginary world, it may well represent not what the authorial audience believes but rather what the author is trying to educate his or her audience into believing. (414)

He thus claims, on the one hand, that there is no necessary correlation between assertion and the beliefs of the authorial audience. On the other hand, he asserts that silence on a central issue indicates that authors expect their readers to be already aware of it. An author's expectation may be the outcome of his or her real or rhetorical assumptions. To decipher whether authors are in complicity with what they think the authorial audience believes or not, we have to understand their rhetorical and conventional assumptions. Rabinowitz suggests that we "can usually separate rhetorical assumption from real assumption . . . by examining the text itself to see if the apparently assumed knowledge or belief in fact plays a role in the development of the [text]" (415). Thus, though readings based on such assumptions are difficult, they may be accomplished if we check the inferences against the role they play in the development of the fiction. But though the text serves as a guide in our determination of rhetorical assumptions, it is "less reliable" in the case of conventional assumptions. Since these assumptions are concerned with "what the authorial audience knows not as 'facts' about the external world but as facts about the literary tradition, regarding what it has learned not from experiences in the world but from experiences with other texts," they function as assertions that define the narrative audience (415). Finally, Rabinowitz asserts that since we learn more from assumptions than from assertions, we should study the context within which conventions operate to determine the relation between texts and "reality."

Following Rabinowitz, I argue that Lawrence's assumptions (or silences) about unmarried women underlying his texts must be valued over his assertions about his contribution to the woman's cause. Nevertheless, Lawrence's representations of unmarried women are complex. While he concurs with essentialism and with the patriarchal attitudes of his culture and blames women for disrupting the natural order of things, he also depicts women as victims, suffering under a patriarchal order that is out of joint. This victimization of women is evident in a story such as "You Touched Me," where, on the one hand, Lawrence shows himself the essentialist and exposes his cultural bias against unmarried women. In this story, though Lawrence equates Hadrian with a rat, Hadrian is "victorious" at the end when he succeeds in silencing Emmie's efforts to oppose his marriage to Matilda; Lawrence upholds his cultural bias against unmarried women and in favor of the heterosexual relation and the feminine mystique.[10] On the other hand, even as Lawrence apparently concurs with past representations of unmarried women in culture and literature, he also experiments in his construction of these characters in ways that capture the patriarchy maintaining its stronghold and, from a feminist perspective, maintaining it insidiously. This experimentation thus allows us to question the stereotypical patriarchal definition of these characters as victims. Though tentative in the short stories, it is more evident in the short novels. There, Lawrence exploits different settings to progress from a secular to a religious vision. In *The Fox*, for example, the lesbian relation of March and Banford is explored in farmyard surroundings and, revealing the threat this poses to the patriarchy, unmasks the weakness in patriarchy that admits this threat. Finally, in *The Escaped Cock*, in which Lawrence culminates his vision with the presentation of a heterosexual union, using a temple setting, the image of Madeleine explodes the madonna-whore binary, releasing her from a polarity within which women have been culturally bound.

IV

Therefore, despite functioning within a binary world-view and within a social system that primarily affirms heterosexual relations, Lawrence remains interesting to feminists and others engaged in cultural critique because his fiction consistently explores alternatives to cultural stereotypes even as it veers back into them, most often, in the end. Moreover, this exploration culminates in an androgynous vision and, in the process, reveals that which otherwise remains concealed. But this androgynous vision is problematic. The problem surrounding Lawrence's vision of androgyny is partly the result of the critics' scepticism about accepting a vision that contradicts his politics of the male and the female.[11] Their scepticism is rooted in the fact that androgyny has often been marshalled in the interests of the male—that is, the male writer colonizes the feminine, getting to be both male and female, while the female isn't allowed to be male. Romantic/Victorian notions of the (male) artist as feminine are exemplary of this. But as opposed to the scepticism of some critics, others find in androgyny a resolution of binaries. For instance, to Carolyn Heilbrun androgyny offers a union of male and female difference within a single being and allows individuals the choice of who and what they want to be (xi-xii). But since union implies fusion and since physical boundaries defy such closure, androgyny has been criticized for being too abstract. Postmodernist approaches to literature, however, more tolerant of difference, explore alternatives and leave room for androgyny understood psychologically. Alexandra Kaplan and Joan Bean see in androgyny a balance between male and female characteristics (defined as psychological androgyny). They contend that androgyny does not require the fusion of physical boundaries between the male and female. According to them, such a bridging is not only impossible but unnecessary, for it is thought that androgyny may now result when a female or male learns how to unite the gender differences within her- or himself. This "union of masculine and feminine," according to Kari Weil, expresses "the dialectical synthesis of what is objectively known (identified as the masculine) and the unknown Other (identified as feminine) who will make that knowledge complete" (2). Kaplan and Bean describe androgynous individuals as those "who are capable of behaving in integrative feminine and masculine ways, who are assertive and yielding, independent and dependent, expressive and instrumental" (2).

Among Lawrence's works, *The Escaped Cock* demonstrates how such a union may be achieved. In this work, the androgyny Lawrence moves toward, though tenuous, is yet an affirmation of the possibility of harmony between female and male within each individual. In *The Escaped Cock*, this union is shaped in mythical terms. Moreover, this final resolution of the male and female differences in the union between the principles of Christ and Pan in *The Escaped*

Cock, though mythopoeic in nature, is consistent with Lawrence's persistently essentialist religious vision of the male-female relation.[12] Though many feminist critics question that religious vision, accusing it of being abstract and contradicting his emphasis on the heterosexual, my study does not concur with such questioning. I believe that to limit ourselves to Lawrence's secular vision is to read only half his story. A symbolic reading of Lawrencean myths and concession to his belief in Christ's humanity contribute greatly to our understanding of his religious vision. In my study, I argue that Lawrence's religious vision is problematic because his fiction suggests that the union of the female and male principles within an individual is only an *initial* step toward the "real" union between the female and the male. Thus, though *The Escaped Cock* offers psychological androgyny, it does not culminate in the presentation of female characters in androgyny. The story of *The Escaped Cock* continues in "The Risen Lord," an essay published posthumously in *Phoenix II*. In this essay, Lawrence asserts the humanity of Christ. Here, he discusses how the man who died rose to marry and have children. It is apparent, however, that Lawrence is able to view women (here Christ, as "the man who died," is representative of the female principle) only within a heterosexual relation. Because Lawrence ends his fiction and essay with the portrayal of a heterosexual union between "the man who died" (or the risen man) and the woman of Isis rather than the celebration of androgyny as represented in Madeleine's transformation from prostitute to madonna, and the transformation of "the man who died," or Christ-crucified to "the risen man," or Christ-resurrected, critics often question the relation between Lawrence's gender and vision.

***

In my study, by focusing on unmarried women, I hope to draw them center stage into a history within which they have hitherto remained invisible and silent. Like Adrienne Rich, I believe that their silence does not signify a necessary absence; rather, their silence speaks volumes about their presence in culture and patriarchy and a story yet to be told. To tell this story, we often need to adopt a position separate from that of the main characters in the narratives. By adopting this new position, my study corrects previous androcentric points of view. It therefore shows that only by telling the story of the unmarried female characters, by “trusting the tale” and not the “teller,” can we excavate a more complete meaning of the Lawrencean text.

Chapter 2

The Short Stories: Part I

Because Lawrence's short stories often focus on a female character as she situates herself, or is situated by outside forces, within the marriage relation, they serve as propaganda for marriage and the feminine mystique.[13] Studies that focus on such a female character promote Lawrence's propaganda for marriage as the norm; thus, they marginalize those female characters who do not marry because they deviate from the norm. For this purpose, I focus on those female characters who remain unmarried at the end of a story and give no indication of marriage in the future. For the sake of convenience, my study is divided into two parts. In this chapter I present part one of my argument by focusing on the older unmarried female characters: namely, Winifred in "The Witch a la Mode," Hilda, Bertha, and Emma in "The Christening," Emmie (and Matilda) in "You Touched Me," Miss James in "The Last Laugh," and Miss Wrexall in "Two Blue Birds."

Since earlier biographical studies of the Lawrencean oeuvre, above all else, center on understanding the psyche of Lawrence through his presentations of the male-female relation, the voice of the unmarried female characters, especially in the short stories, has been silenced. Indeed, past critical discussions surrounding these unmarried female characters have been limited by the influence of Lawrence's ideas about women and the sexual relation between man and woman.

For instance, Widmer uses Lawrence's contempt for Dante, Beatrice, and the ethereal aspect of love to comment that for Lawrence sexual denial implies a "total failure of personality" because without sex "there can be no real passion between man and woman" (131). In his biographical study of Lawrence (1991), John Worthen, in acknowledging the limitations of past criticism on Lawrence, explains that Lawrence's works tend to present the female influences in his life (such as Jessie Chambers, Louie Burrows, and Helen Corke) in one-dimensional terms. Consequently, past Lawrencean critics portray his works as an over-simplification of his life.[14] Following Worthen, I believe that reading the Lawrencean text as an illustration of his ideas or of the events of his life is not enough; to understand his portrayal of the female characters more completely we also need to see them in relation to the social history of unmarried women.

My study of the unmarried female characters in relation to unmarried women in history and in theory at the time Lawrence wrote reveals, primarily, their status as victims—a concept and a position primarily interpreted hitherto in stereotypical male terms—who have been muted by the imposition of patriarchal speech and acts. But sometimes unmarried female characters uphold patriarchy and perpetuate acts against themselves. For instance, my study of "The Witch a la Mode" demonstrates that Bernard Coutts's attitude toward Winifred Varley is similar to the patriarchal attitudes, prevalent during the Medieval and Renaissance times, that persecuted assertive and vocal women (especially unmarried women) for endangering male authority. By equating Winifred with a witch or a "destructive" character, Coutts reduces her to the status of victim in this story. In "The Christening," Lawrence evokes a parallel between Emma Rowbotham and Mary, the mother of Christ, to explore the idea of single motherhood. Through this Biblical association, Lawrence evokes the image of the unmarried woman as the madonna. Yet, within the story, society views Emma as a whore. That this ambiguous vision is resolved in her helpless silence establishes her status as a victim of patriarchy. In "You Touched Me," Lawrence evokes associations of old laws of inheritance to depict the situation of Matilda and Emmie Rockley; whereas private law recognized the right of the unmarried woman to property as equal to that of a man, public law (based on the law of coverture) denied unmarried women this right. Thus, in this story, Matilda and Emmie are victimized by the old patriarchal laws of inheritance. In "The Last Laugh," Lawrence evokes the all-pervasive sense of alienation in post-war

Europe to depict the need for communication in the world. To this end, he coins the metaphor of the laugh of Pan to represent the male principle. The only character able to hear this laugh is Miss James. But Lawrence suggests that James's ability to hear Pan represents her defeat, not her victory. For when she realizes that she is not attracted to a man, she negates her affiliation with Pan. By negating her achievement, the story joins the patriarchy in victimizing a woman by refusing to accept her ability to function without a man. Finally, in "Two Blue Birds," Lawrence evokes Biblical associations of the Creation to present Miss Wrexall, a secretary, as a mute subject who produces in triplicate everything her male "author" speaks. Because Miss Wrexall unquestioningly accepts Mr. Gee's speech and actions, Lawrence demonstrates that she upholds the patriarchy. Thus, Lawrence's representation of unmarried female characters is complex. On the one hand, by juxtaposing the treatment of unmarried women within the Lawrencean oeuvre with their treatment in the past (in culture and in myth), my study demonstrates that Lawrence's representations of women as we find in these stories contradict his claims for the independence of women and suggest that he reinforces images of unmarried women as victims of patriarchy. On the other hand, Lawrence's texts often reveal what is otherwise concealed. Deconstructed, they reveal how insidiously the patriarchy operates to control women's lives and thus exposes a weakness in the patriarchal system.

I

"The Witch a la Mode," begun in 1911 and posthumously published in 1934, revolves around Bernard Coutts, a young man engaged to be married who has a confrontation with Winifred Varley, his former love.[15] One Friday evening, after being away from Croyden for ten months, he visits Mrs. Laura Braithwaite, a young widow. Since Laura's home used to be a meeting place for friends on Friday evenings and was where he had first met Winifred, Coutts knows that he is tempting fate that evening. When Winifred, beautiful and twenty-eight years old, enters with Miss Syfurt (another visitor), the evening proceeds as pleasantly as every other in the past. Later in the evening, by subverting Miss Syfurt's attempt to make them all take the bus on the way home, Winifred manages to remain behind with Coutts. At this time, since she and Coutts have yet to resolve their feelings about their relation, they are unsuccessful when they both try to resist each other. “He hated her, truly. She hated him,” according to the narrator; “Yet they held hands fast as they walked” (63).

As they enter Winifred’s drawing-room, Coutts feels that they enter into surroundings that have remained the same since he was last there, except for a “bowl of magnificent scarlet anemones” on the piano (63). Within these surroundings, though Coutts is attracted to Winifred, he senses her lack of frankness with him and her reluctance to be sexually involved with him. Since he feels inhibited in her presence, he tries to resolve his feelings for her by telling her never to get married. Before he leaves, they embrace and share what he considers her first genuinely given kiss (69). But because Winifred soon withdraws from the kiss, Coutts feels “that she want[s] no more of him than that kiss” (69). He now feels suffocated in her presence, and also feels false to Constance, the woman to whom he is engaged. When he associates the ivory color of a lamp nearby with Winifred, he flies into a rage and lashes out, overturning the lamp. The overturned lamp causes a fire from which Coutts saves Winifred, but even as she clutches at him, he leaves her—she singed but not burnt, he with “burning-red hands held out blindly” (70).

Since the action in this story is often presented through Coutts, it encourages critics to “see” Winifred as he does. Critical commentary surrounding this story thus focuses on two things: first, Lawrence’s use of language to demonstrate Winifred’s attractiveness and, second, Lawrence’s use of metaphors of bewitchment to describe the impact of Winifred’s attractiveness on Coutts. On the first point, critics point out that Lawrence heightens Winifred’s physical attractiveness and reveals Coutts’s response: “Of compact physique, uncorsetted, her figure bowed richly to the piano. He [Coutts] watched the shallow concave between her shoulders, marvelling at its rich solidity” (65). On the second point, critics have noted that Lawrence uses language associated with witches to suggest how Winifred affects Coutts. For example, because Lawrence associates Winifred “with images of brilliance and luster, of fires, candles, crystal, orchids, crocuses” and because “[t]he key adjectives in Coutts’s response to her are aroused, keen, fascinated, intense, exulting, fervid,” Janice Harris suggests that “the arousal, keenness, and fiery intensity he associates with Winifred are tempting, attractive” (51-52). In delineating the relation between Winifred and Coutts, Harris asserts that both are aware of the destructive impact each has on the other; thus, she claims that Winifred is not the victim and Coutts is not the torturer (53-54). But though Harris apportions blame to both the characters and does not overtly equate Winifred with a witch (as do other critics), she discusses the story in terms of the relation between attraction and destruction. She claims that the "linguistic strategy" the couple share, along with the fact that their relation is shrouded in symbolic imagery and language, implies that Coutts and Winifred share only an intellectual energy, not a life-affirming glow, and that "such white-hot intensity is deadly" (52). With this claim, Harris equates beauty and passion with destruction and thus merely follows previous analyses of this story, like those of Kingsley Widmer and Michael Black.

Some critics suggest that because of etymological associations of attractiveness with bewitchment, enchantment, and captivation, Winifred's attractiveness and its impact on Coutts imply that she behaves like a witch.[16] For instance, Widmer views Winifred as displaying the "witchlike destructive power of Woman with her explosive combination of traditional sexual power and modern will" (103). Mistakenly interpreting Coutts as "a married youth," he reads this story as a mere illustration of the adage "that those who play with fire will get burned" so that the final denouement presents the "youthful adulter [sic] . . . running away from the modern witch" (104). Widmer's reading of this story reinforces some of Lawrence's claims about modern women, namely, that "modernity" or assertiveness and independence in women leads to the destruction of civilization ("Do Women Change?" 540). It is unsurprising, therefore, that underlying Widmer's analysis of the story is his view that Coutts's escape from Winifred is an escape from victimization and therefore that his escape is heroic.

Michael Black, like Widmer, views Coutts as a victim who escapes his capture by the witch (Winifred) through heroic endeavor.[17] Through a close reading of the text, Black shows that the things Coutts is enamoured of, such as the train, which is like a "gold-and-black snake," and Winifred's face, which is moon-like, all produce metaphors that suggest Winifred's power to bewitch Coutts. Moreover, when Winifred raises her arms thrice toward Coutts, Black equates her three attempts, through association with ancient and medieval romances, with witchcraft. Black believes that Coutts catapults himself out of his trance by declaring his hatred for trains, as "they pitch one about here and there" ("The Witch a la Mode" 61). Finally, since Coutts (though momentarily lost in the kiss with Winifred) is alerted by the fire and hurries away, Black opines that

Coutts negates Winifred's magic and escapes being victimized. Black thus views Coutts's escape as that of a romantic hero, one "who at the moment of greatest danger undoes the spell by uttering a magic word or performing the right ritual action" (136).

Because past critics "see" Winifred through the lens of Coutts, they equate Winifred with a witch or suggest she has destructive powers. But my study focuses on the *use* of Winifred in the text to reveal that being a "witch" is a bad thing only from the male perspective.[18] From a womanist perspective, her character, in fact, is empowered. For instance, feminists understand that certain kinds of name-calling directed toward women within a patriarchal tradition are devices designed to marginalize and control women. These name-calling practices include those that label women as witches. In "The Witch a la Mode," when Coutts equates Winifred, figuratively, with a witch, this derogatory term provides a means to proscribe her behavior since such terms denigrate women who appropriate agency and establish an independent identity (Penelope xiii-xiv).

Just as misogyny impels the association of attractiveness with witchery, so does it impel calling women names. Julia Penelope, in *Speaking Freely*, claims that these associations (of witches and attractiveness) are apparent when we consider the old relation between language and the treatment of women in history. She refers to *Malleus Maleficarum* or *Hammer of Witches*. Written in the fifteenth-century, this text was accepted as an authority on the inherent evil of women and their consequent treatment during this time.[19] But some since then have agreed with it too. Montague Summers, in his 1928 introduction to *Malleus Maleficarum*, cited misogyny as its underlying theme, but thought it to be a "'wholesome . . . antidote' to the feminism of his time," a time

> when the sexes seem confounded, and it appears to be the chief object of many females to ape the men, an indecorum by which they not only divest themselves of such charm as they might boast, but lay themselves open to the sternest reprobation in the name of sanity and common sense. (quoted in Penelope 25)

Responding to Summers, Penelope claims that misogyny, evident in the book—and in culture at large—is the language of male dominance. Penelope asserts that words are hurtful because languages are far more than words; they invoke systems of rules. Consequently, they depict the power-relation between the people using that language and those on whom the language is used. But in its dangers and the need to be controlled, she explains, language is like a woman. Just as patriarchal descriptions of grammar are credited with magical powers that need to be "controlled" by "rules," so are women credited with magical powers that need to be controlled. In a move favored by deconstructionists, Penelope traces the etymologies of the words "grammar" and "gramarye" to show the deep association of women, grammar, and magic.

> Grammar was borrowed from Latin *grammatica*, "the study of letters" (from Greek *grammatike*). At a later date, *gramarye*, meaning "occult learning" and "magic," was borrowed from French *gramaire* (Old French *grimoire* "book of magic"). The novelist Sir Walter Scott is credited with bringing the Scottish *glamour* ("magic," "spell," with "l" instead of "r") into wide literary use, and etymologists attribute Scott's dialectical variation to a Medieval Latin term, *glomeria*. (xv)

Penelope asserts that associations of magic with language are one way of illustrating "a pervasive way of thinking in English-speaking patriarchies: men perceive both language and women as property that they have the right to control and restrain and the obligation to protect" (xv). She believes that "[m]en's grammatical rules prescribe 'good' English just as their social rules proscribe the behaviors of 'good' women" (xv). Penelope thus suggests that patriarchal attitudes toward witches, or "bad" women, proscribed their behavior through public humiliation. For instance, during the Burning Time in history, which spanned over three centuries from the Medieval to the Renaissance period, women who were accused of being witches because of their power to cast spells, or "glamours," were "tortured, beaten, and burned at the stake" (xv). These spells, it was believed, "caused the genitalia of men to disappear, unmanning them and rendering them impotent, powerless" (xv).

Unmarried women were one of the chief groups of women who bore the brunt of these attacks. Lawrence's work displays the pattern. Like the witches during the Burning Time, Winifred is persecuted by Coutts for her dangerous impact on him. Coutts is attracted by her beauty, but since he is also resentful of its power to attract him and threatened by her constant linguistic challenge, he interprets the power of her beauty and her speech as the power of "glamour," or a spell, over him. Consequently, he tries to undo the spell of this "glamour" by equating her with a witch and "burning" her. Thus, Coutts's treatment of Winifred as a witch follows a long line of such treatment of women by the patriarchy.

Like past indicters, whose cruelty toward women was often the result of their sexual frustration, Coutts indicts Winifred as a witch also because of his sexual frustration. It is clear from one of Lawrence's letters to Edward Garnett in 1912 that not only does he connect magic with women but also that he connects acts of violence with sexual repression. After reading *Jeanne d'Arc*, he wrote, "Cruelty is a form of perverted sex. . . . Priests in their celibacy get their sex lustful, then perverted, then insane, hence Inquisitions—all sexual in origin. . . . It is sex lust fermented makes atrocity" (*Collected Letters* I 156). Just as Coutts knows in the beginning that he is "tempting Providence" ("The Witch a la Mode" 54) and "wilfully" giving "pain to his fiancee" by stopping in Croyden (57), so does he know at the end that he, not Winifred, is responsible for causing the fire. When he equates the ivory of the lamp nearby with the ivory-like looks of Winifred and her unwillingness to continue to kiss him on the mouth, his feelings of frustration catapult him into a rage and he sends the lamp spinning. By causing the fire, he behaves like the indicters during the Inquisition who, fearful of losing their manliness, struck out at those they suspected to be the cause of its loss. Lawrence illustrates Coutts's fear of Winifred by portraying Coutts's reaction to her looks. For instance, from the beginning, Lawrence emphasizes Winifred's ivory-like looks; Coutts symbolically associates her ivory complexion with sexual reticence. Because Coutts is attracted to Winifred and is dissatisfied with her sexual reticence, he expresses his resentment by imposing a terminology of control. Initially, he equates her sexual timidity with a timidity about life itself. By telling her that her behavior is like that of a goddess who can not be touched, he suggests that she is less, not more than, a woman. By telling her that she is merely living voyeuristically by using him as her "Lady-of-Shalott looking glass" (67), he tries to persuade her to have a physical relation with him.[20] But when all his efforts to persuade her fail, he tells her to never marry anyone (68). By suggesting that all men, and not just he, would "see" Winifred's behavior the way he does, Coutts is able to deny the grounds of his own frustration.

Coutts's sexual frustration is most evident in his final encounter with Winifred. Toward the end of Coutts's visit, when Winifred "turn[s] suddenly to meet his full, red mouth in a kiss" (69), Coutts is "[d]azed" by her kiss, and feels "an intolerable ache" in "his overstrained, bursting body" until the hurt brings "him out of the reeling stage to distinct consciousness" (69). At this moment, Coutts believes that like the anemones on her piano, her personality acquires "scarlet" overtones. Under these circumstances, when Winifred alters the embrace to offer her neck, rather than her mouth, to be kissed, Coutts believes that she has "clipped her lips" against him (69). He also believes that just as the anemones were an atypical choice of flowers for her (63-64), so is her kiss on the mouth an atypical act, given her character. Consequently, he interprets her withdrawal from the kiss as a withdrawal from him: he "knew that she wanted no more of him than that kiss" (69). But Coutts's physiological reaction to Winifred's alteration of the embrace ("[h]is whole body ached like a swollen vein" [69]) makes it clear that the sexual frustration he experiences at that moment contributes largely to his labelling Winifred's behavior as unnatural. Coutts must rationalize his sexual frustration and defeat. He needs to *disguise* rejection and represent it as *her* problem rather than his.

Coutts's attraction to Winifred reveals that the witch from whom he escapes to freedom is a projection of his inner desires. That is, when he escapes from "her," he escapes not from an individual, but from himself and the woman in himself. In the beginning, when he resents the "power" of Winifred's attraction over him, he blames her for it: "He was in a position where he was not himself, and he hated her for putting him there, forgetting that it was he who had come, like a moth to the candle" (60). At the end, by considering Winifred's behavior unnatural, he can more easily accept his own moth-like inability to abandon a fire (a figurative representation of his attraction for Winifred) that obviously attracts him and even singes him, but of which he is so afraid that he escapes from it in a sprint.

Lawrence, too, recognized the "power" of attraction as represented in a kiss. To him, a kiss on the mouth represented more than a physical act; it signified an entire philosophy of feeling. In a letter to Blanche Jennings in 1908, he wrote: "Such a touch is the connection between the vigourous flow of two lives. Like a positive electricity, a current of creative life runs through two persons, and they are instinct with the same life force—the same vitality . . . [—]when they kiss on the mouth" (*Collected Letters* I 40). Coutts feels such "electricity" when Winifred kisses him, but is afraid of its power: "Coutts felt a vague fear of Winifred." Lawrence tells us, for instance, "She was intense and unnatural—and he became intense and unnatural, beside her" ("The Witch a la Mode" 65). Therefore blaming his desire to escape on her behavior after Winifred withdraws from kissing Coutts, he looks down at her and interprets her withdrawal as an "unnatural ebb of passion" (69). Consequently, Coutts's escape from Winifred at the end is not heroic (as Black asserts), but, in fact, indicates his own fear and inability to face life and its upheavels.

Feminists reject Coutts's interpretation of Winifred's inability to sustain the kiss on the mouth as a metaphor for her suppressed sexuality. Likewise, they see his interpretation as a metaphor for the suppression of her speech. To them, the mouth suggests the figurative mouth of the vagina—the center of female expression.[21] In this story, just as Coutts deliberately misinterprets Winifred's sexuality, so does he deliberately misinterpret her linguistic ability. Further, just as Coutts's feelings of sexual frustration impel him to label Winifred's shifting of the embrace from a kiss on the mouth to a kiss on the neck as "an unnatural ebb of passion" (69), so his feelings of inadequacy when he is unable to best Winifred at their linguistic games propel him to impose himself on her finally by his departure. Since Winifred can no longer respond to him, his departure imposes a final silence on their "talks."

As opposed to Harris, who believes that Winifred and Coutts's linguistic strategies reduce their relation, I believe that their ability to follow each other indicates their equality in this relation. But because of Winifred's ability to follow Coutts's linguistic strategies, Coutts feels vulnerable to her speech and tries to redress the balance by imposing his speech on hers. From the beginning, speech figures as a key element in Coutts and Winifred's relationship, and both of them share a mutual understanding of the other's linguistic strategies. For instance, Winifred understands that Coutts's hatred of trains is an expression of his hatred of change (61). At this time, because "nothing seems to matter" any more to Coutts, he is briefly able to ignore her "sarcasm" when she sees through him (61). He even agrees with her when she says that he appears to be complaining because he has no troubles in his life. But, soon, because he is unable to determine her response, his resentment impels him to be angry with, and hate, her. When Winifred tells Coutts that "one is never at peace with oneself till one understands," he asks her, "brutally," to explain herself. Arrogantly, he assumes he "*kn[ows]* she *mean[s]* that she *want[s]* to understand the situation he and she [are] . . . in" (my italics 62). Therefore, when Winifred says she wants to understand "[h]ow to resolve the discord," Coutts believes that she is "balking the issue," because "[h]e would have liked her to say: 'What you want of me'" (62). This exchange demonstrates that not only can Winifred follow Coutts, but she, too, can speak as he does. Though Coutts tries to establish the difference between their speech by defining her speech as symbolic, "foggy," or unclear as opposed to his own more clear and direct speech, the fact that he is able to follow her symbolism undercuts his response. Moreover, Winifred indicates to him the symbolic nature of his own speech when he explains that he is like a moth who wanders "blind" and "by instinct" (62). No longer able to ignore her sarcasm, Coutts knows that he "hate[s] her" even though he tells her that they "are just the same as [they] . . . were a year ago" (63). His laughter at this moment is his attempt to cloak his feelings of hatred (63). He feels a return of this hatred when Winifred sneers at his decision to marry Constance as a decision based on instinct. Since he believes that she only likes a "wild-goose chase," and withdraws when he draws near (67), he accuses her of using him as a "Lady-of-Shalott looking glass," and then hates her once again for defining his speech as symbolic and unclear. Though they appear to have reached an impasse in their relation, Coutts resolves it when, moments later, he figuratively silences her by equating her with a witch, and then by running away from her. By equating her with something unnatural, he suggests that her decision to alter the nature of their embrace—from a kiss on the mouth to a kiss on the neck—is unnatural. Following Coutts, at the end we see Winifred as a woman who convulsively "clutch[es] him, almost strangl[es] him, though she . . . [makes] no sound" (70). She tries to catch him even when he moves away. These actions suggest to the reader Winifred's weakness and inability to be independent. They also suggest that Winifred may well have spent the ten months' lapse between Coutts's visit waiting for the drama of her life to begin. But, in fact, at the end, unable to control his attraction for Winifred or her ability to "read" him, Coutts ends their "dialogue" by refusing to participate in it any more.

By fleeing to a woman with whom Coutts feels more in control, he escapes from a woman who is not merely an expression of his desires, but is also a projection of his fears. Briefly, the exchange between Winifred and Coutts demonstrates that Coutts is aware of *his* withdrawal from life. In the beginning, trains possess a snake-like charm for Coutts to which he feels attracted. But later he expresses a hatred for trains. Winifred reminds Coutts that because trains pitch us around they represent change, a condition Coutts had always preferred in the past. While Coutts correctly interprets Winifred's reference to change as a reference to life, he says that he now wishes to be stationary. Despite liking life, he would now like "to be nailed to something, if it was only a cross" (61). But Coutts's desire to be the "willing victim" and play Christ does not affirm his character. For the love he's willing to die for (Constance) is the one who empowers him (64), whereas the love that he rejects (Winifred) is the one who threatens to negate him (60). Indeed, Coutts's decision to marry Constance reveals two things about him. First, in Christian terms, the decision reveals that Coutts's desire to play Christ is blasphemous. For though Coutts is willing to sacrifice himself to Constance—just as Christ sacrificed himself for the masses—Coutts knows that in his relationship with Constance he shall be in control. Second, the decision emphasizes Coutts's awareness of his inferiority to Winifred. For even as he accuses Winifred of not participating in life, his thoughts reveal a greater fear of lived experience within himself:

> With Connie he felt the old, manly superiority; he was the knight, strong and tender, she was the beautiful maiden with a touch of God on her brow. . . . She should rule him later on—that part of him which was hers. But he loved her, too, with a pitying, tender love. . . . Vaguely he knew she would bore him. And Winifred fascinated him. He and she really played with fire. . . . Coutts felt a vague fear of Winifred. She was intense and unnatural—and he became unnatural and intense, beside her. (64-65)

Androcentric readings that revolve around Bernard Coutts, the male character focalizer in the story, are thus unjust in dismissing Winifred as a figure like the Lady of Shalott or a witch.[22] Since "The Witch a la Mode" is not merely a story about Coutts's confrontational meeting with his former love, but is also a story about Coutts's attempt to resolve his feelings—past and present—about Winifred, the fire at the end is not one from which Coutts escapes, but one at which he, afraid to meet the challenge that Winifred represents, burns his "witch." Read from a womanist perspective, however, we question Coutts' designation of Winifred as a witch. In fact, the story is quite remarkable in that it creates a female character strong enough to reject the advances of the male protagonist. The story thus reveals the way in which the patriarchal system operates against the unmarried female in order to retain its self-control.

II

"The Christening," written in 1912 and published in 1914, revolves around Emma Rowbotham's humbling experience as an unwed mother—the worst situation, perhaps, in which a woman in patriarchy can find herself. When this youngest daughter[23] of a puritanical ex-miner has a child by the local baker's man, her father "cease[s] to consider her, since she ha[s] become humbled" (277). Bertha, the middle sister, twenty-eight years old, also talks "sharp[ly] and abrupt[ly]" with Emma. "She scorn[s] her sister, and treat[s] her like dirt" (279). Only Hilda, the eldest sister, unwed and almost thirty, feels Emma's shame, but is ultimately unable to alleviate it either in front of the town's people or at home during the child's baptism. During the private ceremony, which is held at home, both Rowbotham and the clergyman dominate the action. Through their sermons, they try to justify the child's birth as part of God's plan. But in their concern to justify the existence of the child, they forget the mother of the child.

Robert Con Davis, among other critics, argues that "one comes to literary texts to find and take hold of the father" (quoted in Yaeger and Kowaleski-Wallace x). Enacting this argument, many critics of Lawrence focus on understanding the significance of authority in this story. For instance, while Harris claims that in this story Lawrence tries to understand the "crude and powerful father" (79), Widmer claims that the confrontation between Rowbotham and the cleric displays "the irrelevance of the Christian ethos" (27). Both critics, however, overlook the significance of the mother in the text.[24]

Though these critics validate their studies of patriarchal authority by tracing its origin and civilization to Greek myth, Patricia Yaeger and Beth Kowaleski-Wallace, among other feminists, discard the relevance of this mythic universe today (ix). Following these latter critics, while recognizing the influence of such myths to a modernist like Lawrence, I argue for the discovery of the mother's centrality in this text. Accordingly, as opposed to studies that focus on male speech in this story, I focus on understanding the origin and significance of the infantile paralysis and silence of the female characters.[25]

The constant confrontation between the patriarchal discourse, seen as either jeering such as the baker's and brother Laurie's or as condescension such as Rowbotham's and the clergyman's, and the lack of women's discourse highlights the uneven distribution of human power and agency in this story. In feminist terms, this lack of female discourse is related to the well-documented fact that women's history has largely been one of gaps and silences. Tillie Olsen describes some of the "silences [as an] incomplete listing of the incomplete, where the need and capacity to create . . . [are] of a high order" (*Silences* 11). Adrienne Rich, in *On Lies, Secrets, and Silence*, also explains that women's contributions in the past, in both culture and literature, have been disregarded or undervalued (13). But new feminist readings have begun to name the silences that have accompanied women's lives for centuries. Among others, literary critics such as Kate Millett and social critics such as Mary Cadogan and Patricia Craig trace the impact of patriarchy in women's history. While Millett defines this history as one of sexual politics, of a dialectic between male domination and female submission, Cadogan and Craig trace the impact of the two world wars on the victimization of women (and of children). They assert that "[i]n occupied Europe . . . the war reduced many women and children to the status of victims" by marginalizing their function in society (13). In "The Christening," both sexual politics and the impact of the impending war on women coalesce in the imposition of a patriarchal law (secular and religious) that reduces the grown Rowbotham women to the status of children.[26]

The reconstruction of such a persistently restrictive religious and social structure exposes the stark reality of the plight of the Rowbotham sisters, especially Emma. Though all three of the unmarried sisters are assertive women (their volatile interaction with each other suggests their strong personalities), during the christening their most dominant sentiments are resentment, anger, and shame. Though the story focuses on Emma, who "had a downcast, humble mien that sat unnaturally on her" ("The Christening" 275), her two older unmarried sisters are also affected by her predicament. Bertha, the second sister, is a little older than Emma. Significantly, she lacks respect for her sister. "'Good gracious!' exclaimed Bertha. 'You needn't starve the child now you've got it'" (277). But she is extremely gentle toward the child, for "the infant . . . [is] a streak of light to her" 279). Her over-protective attitude toward the child, coupled with the fact that she is the child's godmother, suggests that her ceaseless insults to Emma may be the result of envy of, rather than anger toward, her sister. By constantly putting Emma down, Bertha, like the other women of the town, successfully conveys a lack of sisterhood among women, and thus upholds old patriarchal attitudes toward unwed mothers. But though Bertha remains unsupportive toward Emma and upholds patriarchy, she, too, remains silent under patriarchal law. For instance, Bertha, along with Emma, quietly kneels during Rowbotham's sermon (281).

In contrast to Bertha, Hilda, a schoolmistress, feels Emma's shame and feels protective toward the baby and its mother. Lawrence suggests that like Bertha's, Hilda's status as an unmarried woman, too, influences her attitude toward Emma. For instance, in the beginning, we are told that to the colliers's wives her heart disease and general frailty have sealed her fate as an unmarried woman. Lawrence writes, for example, that two women hurrying home "to scramble their husbands' dinners together" grimace at her "ridiculous" figure (274). But her relative youth (she is not yet thirty), her comely appearance (274), and her protective love for the baby (279), suggest that she, too, may have harbored desires for a relationship and a child despite her suffering from heart disease. Further, though Hilda never refers to the child, she is unable effectively to express her support to her sister, privately, or, in front of others. For instance, on the day of the christening, though she speaks out for her sister, she fails to defend her from the baker's indifference. There, her "rapid and nervous speech" (274) in contrast to the "churlish[ness]" (274) of Mr. Berryman, the baker, establishes a hierarchical relation between them. Though she is a grown working woman of thirty, initially, "[h]er lips flutter . . . like two leaves in a wind, and her words crowd . . . and rush . . . like a flock of sheep at a gate," when she talks to the baker (274). Responding to his churlishness with irony, she pretends to accept that one can not always have what one wants and thus obliquely refers to her sister's predicament. But when she tells Mr. Berryman that spoiling oneself is "less profitable . . . than trying to spoil somebody else" (274-75), he merely looks glumly back at her. Her irony is lost on Mr. Berryman; it merely confuses him. Even when he questions Hilda about Emma, he directs his question "to the flour-scoop" (275). Angered by this objectification of her sister, Hilda challenges him to mention her sister by name. But by referring to Emma as "[t]he youngest" (275), he ignores her challenge. Though Hilda is angered by his indifference and tells him with "sharp ironical defiance" (275) that Emma is fine, she leaves his shop in great embarrassment. Though Hilda carries home with her a "white bag with an appearance of steadfast unconcern" (275), her attempt in this exchange to dominate the baker with her middle-class dignity remains unsuccessful. Moreover, because her ironic speech is reduced to insignificance by Berryman's inability or refusal to comprehend her, she remains powerless to erase her sister's "mark" of shame, and yields to the baker power to continue his verbal harrassment.

Throughout the story, though Hilda feels Emma's shame, she resents its "mark upon the family" (279). Her feelings impel her, initially, to keep her distance from her sister (275) and, later, to speak "sharply" to her rather than to their brother, Laurie, when he mocks Emma. Unable to tolerate Emma's belligerance at their brother's jeering remarks, she exclaims to Emma in reference to the pregnancy and child, "Good gracious, it hasn't improved your temper" (282). This exclamation of impatience suggests that Hilda, like Bertha, blames Emma for her predicament and, as a result, expects quiet submission from her. Also like Bertha, Hilda is silenced by patriarchal speech, as she was in the beginning when, though resentful of the baker's indifferent queries about Emma, she is silenced by his refusal to comprehend her irony. Later, though resentful of her father's "discourse," she is silenced by the unleashing of his anger. Before the christening, Hilda sits "exceedingly nervous" at the table and talks "in little volleys" while her "hands flutter" (279). During the baptism, as "the lady of the family," she sits "stiff and pained [,]. . . at a loss before her father's religious sentiment." She resents "bitterly the mark upon the family, against which the common folk could lift their fingers" (279). Bertha's and Hilda's behavior in front of the two "fathers" suggests that though both of them are also subject to patriarchal authority, they, in turn, subject Emma to their authority. In other words, not only are they victimized by the patriarchy, but they, in turn, uphold patriarchy and victimize Emma. In feminist terms their attitude parallels what Sandra Gilbert explains as the problem of daughterhood with which every woman writer is faced. If we accept Gilbert's terminology, then we could say that when Hilda and Bertha are faced with Emma's deviant behavior, they are faced with "the riddle of daughterhood, a figurative empty pack." For the older sisters, "the terror of the female precursor"—Emma, in this case—"is not that she is the emblem of power but, rather, that when she achieves her greatest strength, her power becomes self-subverting" (357). Further, explains Gilbert, "in the moment of psychic transformation that is the moment of creativity," the female precursor becomes the "'stern daughter of the voice of God' who paradoxically proclaims her 'allegiance to the law' she herself appears to have violated" (357).

Anger overwhelms Emma when her sisters direct her actions, when she hears her father justify her child's existence, when the clergyman fumbles for sufficiently benign sentiments to utter, and when she tries, physically, to silence her brother's jeering. But though Emma's feelings of anger and her past relationship with the baker's man suggest her strength of character, her mettle, ironically, becomes the cause of her "shame." Worse, it is magnified by the lack of sisterhood among the women and keeps her silent in the presence of everybody. On the day of the christening, we are told that though she has a "downcast, humble mien," this humility sits "unnaturally on her" (275). Hurt by everyone's treatment of her, she reacts with irritation and anger to them all. For instance, initially, irritated by her father's clumsiness when he drops a piece of coal on the hearth, she turns on him in a "rough, loud voice of anger," but quickly and "consciously moderate[s] . . . her tones" (276). When Rowbotham tries to remedy his slip and hurts himself, Emma is angered by his further clumsiness. This time she speaks "roughly" to him and pushes "him into his chair." Attracted by this exchange, Bertha scolds Emma for speaking disrespectfully to their father and "command[s her] sharply" to fetch some medicine for him. Also ordering Emma to feed the child, she thus implies that Emma is incapable of taking care of her responsibilites toward child or father. Though Emma sets aside her kitchen tasks to take care of her father and child, her "obedience," says Lawrence, is "more intolerable than the most hateful discord" (276).

Emma's feelings of "anger" and "bondage" when she listens to the male "discourse"—with the arrival of Mr. Kendal, the cleric, to conduct the baptism—make evident her status as victim in a patriarchal society. Though the cleric disrupts the picture of domestic disharmony, he is unable to alleviate their pain and is at a loss for words in front of Emma. Seeing her breast-feed her child, he “softly and gently” asks her how she is. He speaks as though “she were ill and he were mindful of her.” Though Emma feels “anger” at his question, she controls her feelings enough to take his hand “awkwardly” and tell him that she’s all right (278). Having exchanged preliminary greetings, the cleric feels “lost in a deep musing.” Looking down at the child sucking at his mother’s breast, he can only repeat himself, “Yes—Yes . . . Yes, Yes” (278). When he comes out of his reverie, he is still incapable of sensible action; therefore, he shakes hands with Emma “unseeingly” (278). Though the cleric’s presence at the private ceremony suggests his support of the family in general and Emma in particular, his manner at their home suggests his discomfiture with his position. By treating Emma “unseeingly,” he mimics the attitude of Rowbotham during the baptism. Rowbotham’s sermon about God’s culpability in the child’s birth angers Emma even more than does the cleric’s need to “not see” her. At this time, Emma is

> hurt, and a little glowering anger sh[ines] in her face. But nevertheless her fingers clasp . . . the body of the child beautifully. She . . . [is] stupefied with anger against this emotion let loose on her account. (279)

Not only does Emma feel belittled by the atmosphere preceding the ceremony, but her son’s baptism ceremony makes her victimization even more intolerable. During the ceremony, Emma sits silent while Hilda presides and Bertha takes care of the domestic concerns. After the sermon, when the child is baptized and they all kneel down to pray in “relief,” Emma feels only a desire to hide herself. At this moment, looking up, she sees her brother’s grinning face though the window. While she sits “still[,] . . . anger . . . fill[s] her heart. She . . . hate[s] now the praying clergyman and the whole emotional business; [and] she hate[s] her brother bitterly” (280). The report of a burst paper bag effectively brings the ceremony to an end, and Emma hurries into the scullery to question Laurie. But Laurie torments her by tipping the child under his chin and singing a nursery song about a baker. Since Emma’s lover is baker’s man at Berryman’s, Laurie’s song completely humiliates her. She attempts to quiet him, but he merely sings another jeering song. Since neither Emma’s anger nor Rowbotham’s arrival can silence Laurie, Bertha carries the baby away while Hilda scolds Emma for not being more improved in temper by her experience.

The behavior of the elder sisters suggests that since Emma has done "wrong," she may be "sullen and furious" (282), but she will not be able to quiet the world and, therefore, must be quiet herself. Her silence does not empower her. Rather, because it is imposed by the speech of the two "fathers" and by the baker's man's silence, it represents, like her child, a mark of her shame. Indeed, Emma's shame is by gender association the shame of her sisters; thus, the silence of all three women in the presence of the men, as Kramarae's study of such male speech and female silence suggests, represents their subordinate status in patriarchal society (1).

Lawrence represents both male silence and speech, both of the baker's man and of the two "fathers" regarding the baker's man, as empowering to them. The text reveals that while Emma has to endure societal chastisement, male silence about the baker's man protects him. Significantly, not only do both the "fathers"—Rowbotham and the clergyman—try to control the meaning of Emma's unwed motherhood by claiming distance from it, but they also, in the course of their sermonising, fail to refer to male responsibility. In other words, we never hear about the culpability of the baker's man. For example, in the case of Rowbotham, Lawrence demonstrates that from the beginning, he is either unable or simply refuses to understand his daughter's predicament. The only way he can understand her situation is by elevating it to religious proportions and by seeing it as part of God's plan. "Lord, when a man says he is a father, he is wrong from the first word. For Thou art the Father, Lord" (280). Able by this act of faith to transfer the responsibility of fatherhood from his shoulders to God's, Rowbotham is thus able to accept the absence of the child's natural father. So transferring the responsibility of fatherhood, Rowbotham, in effect, transfers "blame" to God and portrays himself as an obedient, if ignorant, follower of God's ways. As he says, "I don't like leavin' a girl o' mine in a situation like 'ers is, but what the Lord's done, He's done, an' it's no matter murmuring" (279). Like Rowbotham, even the clergyman, a man devoted to service and who one might expect to have more love and forgiveness in his heart, is capable of feeling only "a kind of unreal love . . . [since h]e had never mixed with life, and women were all unliving, Biblical things to him" (280). Not only is the clergyman unable to relate to Emma, but he is also unable to sympathise with Rowbotham. Because "unaware of the feelings of a father[,] . . . [he hears] without understanding the special language of fatherhood" (281).

By refusing to acknowledge Emma's "reality," the two "fathers" suggest that her predicament is similar to that of the Madonna. But by expressing their need to promote this image in the privacy of the home, the "fathers," conversely, suggest that she is a whore. In the beginning, the title of the story combines with the religious tone of the text to evoke memories of another such birth in Bethlehem. But soon we realize that the story explores the ambivalent attitude of the patriarchy toward virginity. In patriarchal societies, says Millett in her reconstructive and anthropological study of women in patriarchal structures of organization, virginity is perceived as both a symbol of property and a representative of the unknown other that is to be feared; thus both worth and worthlessness are associated with virginity (74-82).

By conjuring associations of the woman as both the madonna and the whore, "The Christening" conjures a stereotype of the binary choices within which women have been circumscribed by culture and one of its agents, literature. Thus, the cleric's inability to understand Emma, who as a woman is an "unliving, Biblical thing to him," not only mirrors the efforts of the biological father to elevate her experience to a position similar to that of the madonna, but it also evokes associations with the subversion of women virtually throughout history for expressing their sexuality.[27]

We therefore see that just as in "The Witch a la Mode" Winifred Varley is treated like a witch by Bernard Coutts, in "The Christening," Emma Rowbotham is treated like a whore, or an emblem of shame by the patriarchy for daring to express her sexuality. It is understandable, then, why the cleric can extend to Emma only the wooden comfort that time is a great healer and that the birth of a male child is cause for rejoicing. Appropriate within a patriarchal structure, such joy suggests that the child's gender shall at least eliminate the possibility of repetition of their current shame. Further, since a child is commonly associated in culture and literature as a symbol of hope, the mark of the covenant between humankind and God, the child, through Biblical association, is thus emblematized in Christ, the son of God, the mark of God's promise to deliver the world from pain and evil.[28] By using the metaphor of the christening, Lawrence emphasizes its contradictory nature. The contradiction inherent in this vision of a promise of happiness in the future despite pain in the present is repeated in the clergyman's solace to the Rowbothams in "The Christening." By focusing on Emma's "shame" rather than on her feelings regarding her predicament or on seeking resolutions to her problem, the "fathers," selfishly, refocus the action from Emma to themselves. But though they try to deny Emma's reality and elevate her to the position of a Madonna, they suggest through their sermons that, for her, redemption lies only in passively accepting the plan of God (the ultimate representative of male law within a Christian worldview).

Emma's shame represents her status as a "fallen" woman. The secrecy shrouding the affair, together with the social condemnation that necessitates the baptism of the child be a private affair, adds to her shame (279). For instance, Emma flushes when the clergyman sees "her *dishonoured* breast . . . uncovered" (my italics 278) while she's feeding her son. Lawrence thus, metonymically, expresses the feeling of social condemnation in Emma's mind. Nor Hall offers a framework in which to understand Emma's feeling of shame at this moment. Hall explores the depiction of the breast in art in the Greek tradition. She discusses how over a period of time a display of flesh degenerated into an embarrassment so that, during the Renaissance period, the Virgin was portrayed as a lady (*The Moon and the Virgin* 53-58). Margaret Miles, in her essay "The Virgin's One Bare Breast: Female Nudity and Religious Meaning in Tuscan Early Renaissance Culture," also discusses the popularity of the paintings of the madonna with one bare breast from the trecento through the next three hundred years. Miles believes that

> [n]udity . . . in religious paintings creates tensions of two kinds. . . . First, there is a tension between cultural and natural meanings. The bare-breasted Virgin . . . evokes visual associations that emphasize her similarity with other women; yet popular devotional texts and sermons frequently contradicted these evoked associations by insisting on her difference. . . . Second, nudity in religious paintings creates a tension between erotic attraction and religious meaning. (203)[29]

The impact of the patriarchal gaze in relation to the painting of the Virgin's bare breast as explained by Miles operates in this Lawrence story as well: When the male cleric looks at Emma's bare breast, she feels dishonor and shame at being an unwed mother rather than pride in her motherhood.

While I do not believe that Lawrence personally upholds Emma's social condemnation, he does make it clear. In agreement with Roland Barthes, I believe that since "[a]ll images are polysemous[,] . . . they imply, underlying their signifiers, a floating chain of signifieds" for us to choose from or to ignore (quoted in Miles 196). The story challenges patriarchy by conflating the image of the madonna and the whore in the portrayal of Emma to explode the myth of the woman as either the one or the other, but the story also suggests Emma's condemnation both by evoking associations between carnality and sin and by depicting her as a silent figure. At the end, though the "slavering" speech of the father irritates his children, who all chafe against it, his "loud voice, with joy in life still," has "some power" that prevails over them all ("The Christening" 282). Despite her inner rage at the patriarchal sermonizing, Emma, in her sullen silence, suggests that no "other" way lies ahead of her, and determines her status as a victim of a patriarchal system that perpetuates its power through religion and blind faith.

III

"You Touched Me," begun in 1919 as "Hadrian" and published under its new title in 1920, focuses on Mr. Rockley's unfair treatment of his two unmarried daughters, Matilda and Emmie.[30] When the story begins, they are "already old maids" (394).[31] Matilda is thirty-two and Emmie is thirty, and neither of them expects to get married. Because of their age and their fortune (each of them will inherit ten thousand pounds), they are socially and economically above all the men they can meet in their industrial town, for "[i]n a thorough industrial district, it is not easy for the girls who have expectations above the common to find husbands" (394).

In the past, since Mr. Rockley, the father of four daughters (two of whom are married), had craved a son, he had adopted a boy of six from a charity institution. Because the girls were adolescents at the time of Hadrian's adoption (Matilda was sixteen and Emmie was fourteen), they were resentful and distant from Hadrian. Hadrian reciprocated this resentment and distance. At the age of fifteen, aloof from and ungrateful to his adoptive family, Hadrian ran away to the colonies, only to return suddenly at the age of twenty-one when Mr. Rockley is dying. Things change with Hadrian's return, for he has always been a favorite with Mr. Rockley. Since the women still sustain their childhood resentment against Hadrian, on his return they continue to keep their distance from him. Events gather momentum when one night, planning to check on her ailing father, Matilda mistakenly enters Hadrian's room and puts her hand on the youth before discovering her mistake. While Matilda regrets her mistake, Hadrian becomes obsessed by her touch and by his desire to possess her. He appeals to Mr. Rockley for help to "get" her. Since Mr. Rockley sees this as yet another opportunity besides adoption to have Hadrian for his son, he is eager to help him out. Therefore, he plots with him against his own daughters. When he threatens to change his will and leave behind his inheritance to Hadrian if Matilda refuses to marry him, he outrages the daughters. But though they articulate their anger to their father as well as to Hadrian, their rage does not affect either of the men.

Since Lawrence, the self-professed priest of love, formulated his theory of an erotics based on touch (Moore, Harry T. 87-8),[32] most biographers and critics of Lawrence focus on his repeated emphasis on tactile communication in this story—a theme that is apparent in the title, "You Touched Me."[33] But they explore this metaphor only to explain further the traditional heirarchical relation between the male and female as they move toward marriage. For example, Widmer suggests that the episode of Matilda's visit to Hadrian's room that night illustrates her unconscious desire for Hadrian (60). Certainly, Widmer's argument offers us one explanation for Matilda's final obedience and submission to both her father's and Hadrian's will. But by focusing on the end result, that is, her marriage to Hadrian, and her submission to Hadrian and her father, these critics concentrate on male victory. Consequently, as they completely overlook the gender implications of her submission, they also completely overlook the other sister's—Emmie's—efforts to avert the crisis. Thus, though the action of the story and its initial title, "Hadrian," suggest Hadrian's manipulation of Rockley and his daughters, critics continue to ignore the way the story reduces the Rockley sisters to the status of victims.[34]

Widmer correctly observes that from the start, Matilda, though as impatient as Emmie at Hadrian's cocky behavior, is more tolerant of it. But I believe that critics such as Widmer, who argue that Matilda's predicament is willful, do not emphasize enough the fact that even Hadrian acknowledges the instigating incident to have been an innocent error. As Hadrian tells Matilda, he knows her visit to his room in the night "was a mistake" ("You Touched Me" 409). But there still seems something between Matilda and Hadrian. In the beginning, for instance, though both Matilda and Emmie are described as plain looking and domesticated (395), when Hadrian arrives suddenly to visit Rockley, Matilda is especially ruffled at being caught unprepared and not fully dressed. Therefore, when Emmie tells her to go up and dress herself, she hastens to do so. Later, when Emmie becomes suspicious of Hadrian's pecuniary motives for visiting the dying Mr. Rockley, Matilda rebukes her sister. Further, when Emmie calls him a "mannie," Matilda replies that "he's not bad" (398). She also tells Emmie that she must not "be prejudiced against him" (398). Even when Hadrian's obvious attempts to blackmail her into marriage anger Matilda, her response to him is ambivalent and confused rather than outright dismissive. The narrator tells us, for example, that "When she remembered . . . [his face under her hand] she was bewildered" (403). Hadrian, aware of her bewilderment, takes advantage of it by holding her responsible for putting thoughts of her in his head when she mistakenly touches him. While he repeatedly refers to her touch as something he can not forget, this "charity boy," who feels controlled by the magical, bewitching "glamour" of Matilda's "common-place kindliness" and "superior breeding" and wants "to make himself master of it" (403), can not forget that the attitude of the Rockley sisters toward him makes him feel "angry," "depressed," and "despised" (409). Toward the end, even after Matilda agrees to marry Hadrian, she turns away from him because she considers herself his superior and therefore "looks down on him both literally and figuratively" (409). At this time, she tries to assert her old feeling of superiority over Hadrian. Refusing to talk to him, she hopes her silence will give her control over him. Even on the day they marry, Matilda still stands "*silent* and *unmoved*" (my italics 409)[;] she is "*quiet*, very *still*" (my italics 410). It is unsurprising, therefore, that Hadrian should find gratification in turning the tables to make her feel "trapped" (409) by his silence. Moreover, Hadrian overturns the old status quo when, in a crucial Lawrencean moment, he forces Matilda to kiss him on the mouth. With this kiss, she relinquishes her control over Hadrian. But this kiss on the mouth does not represent a shared experience of love as Lawrence's assertions about such a kiss suggest,[35] nor does it represent a gesture of peace as stereotypical portrayals of such a kiss in culture and literature illustrate. On the contrary, since the mouth is most obviously associated with speech, the kiss here suggests a figurative act representing the suppression of her speech. Unlike the silence she chooses, her silence now is no longer a silence that gives her control. Therefore, when Rockley (whom she hasn't kissed since she was a child) and Hadrian force Matilda to kiss them, they exhibit her status within a patriarchal society: they show that she's a victim, not a victor.[36]

Hadrian achieves his victory over Matilda by flattering Rockley's vanity. He conspires to "get" Matilda by letting Rockley think that the older man has "got" her for the younger. Carrying out his plan, he first pretends to ask Rockley for approval for marrying his daughter: "I'd marry her," he says, "if you wanted me to" (404). And second, he feeds Rockley's ego by asking him for help. "She'd take more notice of you," he tells Rockley (404). Hadrian's machinations for gaining Rockley's approval thus serve as a means to his success in fooling him and "getting" his daughter. Read "against the grain," the text reveals that these machinations prove not only Hadrian's cleverness, but they also demonstrate how Matilda is made a commodity who is bartered by the father in exchange for a son. One may argue that though Hadrian "gets" Matilda as his wife, old Rockley "gets" him as a son through marriage to his daughter. Although human life is reduced to property in both transactions, Hadrian's reduction ("Ay, my lad, I'm glad you're mine" 410) is presented in terms of a victory over Matilda. "[Y]ou've got her?," Rockley asks Hadrian (410). Matilda's reduction thus constitutes part of Hadrian's victory, for it allows Rockley to think he has got Hadrian when, in fact, Hadrian has got Rockley by acquiring both his daughter and her fortune.

While Matilda finally succumbs to the patriarchal will, Emmie stands alone. From the start, in contrast to Matilda, Emmie's response to Hadrian's arrogance is less tolerant. "Hadrian's new-fledged, cocksure manliness," Lawrence's narrator tells us, "evidently found no favour in her eyes" (398). When we juxtapose Lawrence's views on cocksure women and cocksure men with Emmie as an example of a cocksure woman and Hadrian as an example of a cocksure man, it is relatively easy to understand the struggle between them in the story. Lawrence often claimed that the new or "modern" woman is independent and self-assertive. He called this new woman the "cocksure woman": "A really up-to-date woman is a cocksure woman. She doesn't have a doubt nor a qualm. She is the modern type" ("Cocksure Women and Hensure Men" 552). But though the new woman is cocksure and fights for causes like votes, sports, or welfare, Lawrence claimed that "she is a hen all the time" (555). Thus, he claimed that her cocksureness is only an act. In comparison to the cocksure woman, the cocksure man, as Lawrence describes him, is a "cockerel [who] is, naturally, sure. He crows because he is certain it is day" (552). Since Lawrence's essentialist attitude toward women was determined by his belief that a man's cocksureness is natural and a woman's cocksureness is unnatural, it is unsurprising that this story demonstrates the victory of Hadrian over Emmie too. It is only "natural" that "nature" should prevail.

Lawrence demonstrates Emmie's cocksureness most effectively when she is confronted by her father's threat to change his will. At this time, she is "like a fighter ready to fight to the death" (407). After her initial angry response to the men's manipulation, she advises Matilda not to marry Hadrian, for she feels the two women can look after themselves. Since Matilda is more focused on her personal relation with Hadrian, Emmie feels alone when she learns the extent to which they are subject to the old laws of male inheritance unsympathetic to the woman's plight. A study of these laws shows us that they perpetuate belief in male superiority by arranging the descent of property ownership through the male line (Baker 305). The aspect of property law that "You Touched Me" exploits is the differing status of unmarried and married women in relation to inheritance of property. While private law allowed the unmarried woman to enjoy the same legal privileges as men, in public law she had no rights. In addition, since public law was based on the law of coverture and focused on the unity of husband and wife, it posited that the woman was protected under her husband (Kanowitz 35-41). Further, Kate Millett delineates the slow and partisan nature of the achievement of the Married Woman's Property Act, from 1856 to 1908, to discuss the significance of the change in the legal status of women as an achievement in terms of the women's movement (98). Even after the Married Woman's Property Act had come into existence, in many cases of dispute following judges were still known to follow the rule of "natural male dominance" (Kanowitz 40). Because the Act was in place by the time Lawrence's story was written, "You Touched Me" demonstrates the continued perpetuation of "natural" rule that aggrandizes patriarchy.

Confronted with the law of old Rockley and Hadrian, Emmie asks the solicitor, the clergyman, and relatives to intervene and talk to Hadrian. In other words, she appeals to the law of the land, the church, and society, but to no avail. "You Touched Me," however, is more problematic because of its presentation of male characters as dually willful and helpful. On the one hand, we are presented with the stubborn willfulness of Mr. Rockley and Hadrian; on the other hand, we are presented with the helpfulness of the solicitor and the clergyman. Such disparate behavior by the males demonstrates that the will of the male, in patriarchy, is arbitrary and operates at random, creating the greatest of vulnerability and keeping women off balance. Now a man is kind, now he's brutal, and the woman never knows what it will be or when. Both the latter men's solicitousness, however, is impotent in the face of the father's rights. As a result, the men can only try to change Hadrian's mind; they can not tell the father how to act.

At the same time Lawrence shows how helpful men such as the solicitor and the clergyman can be, he lucidly presents Mr. Rockley's and Hadrian's malevolence toward Matilda and Emmie. "If you won't . . . [agree to my plans,] I'll make you pay for your foolishness" ("You Touched Me" 405), says Rockley to his daughters. What draws our attention to this malevolence, however, is its final victory. Not only does the father's will prevail, but so does Hadrian's. In this context, it is interesting to note that the drama, and the females' ability to act independently, surrounds the question of inheritance and the future in more ways than one. Hadrian, the adoptive son, is to be the keeper of old Rockley's watch (a cultural metaphor for time—past, present and future) and the chain (which keeps the watch, and what it represents, in place). Since time is a "nonspatial continuum," as the inheritor of time, Hadrian's inheritance defies boundaries and does not need to be recorded. "I haven't put his name in the will," Mr. Rockley tells his daughters (401). On the other hand, the daughters' inheritance is to be proscribed within the parameters of the father's "will," which operates both as a legal and a cultural imperative for control. Working within the bounds of this understanding, initially, when their father threatens to change his will, both the sisters stand "pale, *mute*, stubborn" (my italics 407). Even when Emmie tries to impose her speech, and thus her power, over Hadrian by calling him a "demon" (405) and a "guttersnipe" (407), she merely demonstrates her helplessness. For Hadrian is "courageous," albeit like a cornered rat, and so can triumph in the end (407).

Not only does he defeat Matilda and Emmie by prevailing over their right to their father's property, but he also scores victory when he reduces them to silence. But though Hadrian reduces both women to silence, he adopts different ways to accomplish his victory over each woman. While he silences Matilda with the aid of her father and by "blaming" her for touching him and awakening his desire for her, he silences Emmie by ignoring her. By focusing his energies on Matilda, he undermines the significance of Emmie's concerns. He thus dooms to failure Emmie's attempts to be assertive. Not only are her efforts at self-expression silenced by her father's and Hadrian's anger, but, ironically, she can be heard only by appropriating the speech of another male, that is, the solicitor, who is the symbol/father of law, and the clergyman, who is the father to his flock.

But as in "The Christening," so in "You Touched Me," it is the biological father's speech that ultimately prevails (408). Appropriately, then, when Emmie challenges her father about his threats to Matilda, he silences her by shouting to the maid to call the solicitor to change the will. By shouting for Annie, the maid, he demonstrates that though he is on his death bed, he still has "power to make his voice carry" (406). The proscribing effect of male speech and law (which is an expression of male speech) is correspondingly reflected in the women's silence. Only male language, that of logic, is allowed to have meaning. Hence, language is androcentric. Appropriately, then, when Emmie's efforts to be heard are described as "raving" and "weeping" (409), the words merely connote delirium and eliminate sense, reason, power, and agency from an action. Though Emmie attempts to talk with the patriarchy, she is defeated by it. By presenting Emmie as "raving," and by describing both Matilda and Emmie as "old maids" who are rendered "dumbfounded," "mute," and "silent" within a patriarchal culture, Lawrence dramatizes the treatment of women as children. He also dramatizes the lack of women's rights—a social phenomenon that continues to prevail despite its limiting and malevolent intent and despite its subsequent legal end. Lawrence, however, more than records a cultural fact; by presenting Matilda and Emmie as finally silenced under male law, he presents them in the stereotypical terms of victim. This victimization is especially emphasized when the final resolution excludes them and focuses purely on the male victory. But though Lawrence focuses on male victory, his text does not uphold patriarchy, whether wittingly or unwittingly. In fact, by focusing on how the patriarchy strengthens itself by belittling women, we note that in fact the text exposes the weakness of patriarchy, the means to which it must stoop in order to maintain its ascendancy.

IV

"The Last Laugh," written in 1924 and first published in 1925, revolves around the unusual experiences of a woman named James, who is over thirty years old and the daughter of a peer, and a young man, Marchbanks. One dark winter night, as they walk together in the snow after they leave a party, Marchbanks hears somebody laughing. But since James is deaf and is not wearing her hearing aid at the time, she does not hear the laugh. After a while, however, she feels "connected" and can hear the laugh coming from Marchbanks (632). Attracted to the sound of voices, a young policeman joins them. Like James, he, too, can hear only Marchbank's laugh and not the laugh that Marchbanks claims he can hear. Frustrated, Marchbanks disappears into the bushes to try to trace the source of *his* laugh. The others follow him. While James stands waiting by the bushes, she sees a man who may be the source of the laugh. But the policeman does not share her vision. Meanwhile, Marchbanks decides to look behind the trees for the source of the laugh. There, he comes to a house where he is greeted by a young Jewess who welcomes him for the night. When James sees Marchbanks follow the woman inside her house, she decides not to wait for him. Overtaken by a snow storm on her way home with the policeman, she first hears voices and then she hears laughter. As her ability to hear returns to her, James begins to feel independent and free. On ariving home, she permits the policeman to stay downstairs in her living room to warm himself before he leaves. But in the morning James's housekeeper informs her that he is still there, for he has become lame. In no rush to run to his side, she stays up to ponder her relations with men. But with Marchbanks's arrival her reverie is broken and she goes down with him to meet the policeman. Downstairs, just as she hears the strange laugh again, Marchbanks, too, appears to see somebody. But his vision, unlike the vision that released James from deafness, strikes him dead.

Though most critics either ignore or dismiss this story as insignificant, I believe it has great value within the Lawrencean oeuvre. Critics such as R. P. Draper, for instance, dismiss "The Last Laugh" as one in a cluster of "satirical stories" that are "brittle, unformed, and rather jeering in tone" (130). Further, Kingsley Widmer, though finding it part of a literary tradition, dismisses this story for its irrelevance to our world. He claims that using the demonic within the Western tradition, in this story Lawrence employs "the Gothic tricks of his romantic predecessors [to] make . . . effective melodrama" (98). Additionally, Widmer views the demonic device as Lawrence's means to intellectualize and to transcend the ironic.[37] He correctly asserts that, in this story, it is Pan who comes back with his bacchic laughter to "alter the world immediately" ("The Last Laugh" 642), but goes on to state that "Lawrence hasn't provided much world, or character, to be altered; shattering churches, policemen, and intellectuals remain supernatural trickery" (56). In making this evaluation, however, Widmer misses Lawrence's point. I believe that it is precisely because the world that Lawrence presents is one of "shattered churches, policemen, and intellectuals" that there exists a need to alter it immediately. Moreover, it is through the "supernatural trickery" that this story transcends other stories that create a more realistic landscape and characters. Here, though Lawrence is still concerned about a war-torn, increasingly mechanized and godless universe (as he is in many of his works), he is now experimenting with, for him, a new form of writing: allegory. To dismiss this story as Widmer does, therefore, is to miss making a relationship between this allegoric universe and our own.

Though Janice Harris discusses the allegorical significance of this story, she bases her discussion on Lawrence's mythmaking. In brief, Harris responds to the limitations of Widmer's approach by fleshing out the allegory. She claims that, in this story, just as day follows night, Marchbanks is punished with death for getting side-tracked in his search for Pan, the policeman is crippled for his inability to hear, or to believe, in the laugh, and James is herself freed of her dependence on machines when she hears and believes in the laughter. Harris suggests that since Pan's bacchic laughter here represents the life-principle that James embraces and the others ignore or discard (176), James's ability, therefore, represents her victory. (In "The Overtone" Lawrence discusses how he relates Pan to the male principle and Christ to the female principle.[38]) But a reading in line with Harris does not account for why, despite her ability now to communicate with others, James is isolated from them.

To understand James's final isolation, we must extend the limits of Harris' allegoric reading of this story. In this story, Lawrence evokes the atmosphere of a war-torn Europe to show its consequences on humanity and, thus, weaves together two of his favorite themes: an increasing alienation of humankind from the natural universe and the difficulty of the male-female relation within such a universe. Since he claimed that the war had altered the old relation between men and women from man as Christ-child and woman as his "safeguard," to man as Christ-crucified and woman as "manless, bitter or overassertive," he believed that humanity needed to create another image of man in order to re-unite the two sexes ("The Risen Lord" 572-74).[39] In "The Last Laugh," Lawrence explores the consequences of human attempts to communicate when miscommunication is misperceived as communication.

In the beginning of the story, James is deaf. By the end, because she not only can see but also can hear Pan, she is able to communicate better with herself and the outside world and therefore no longer needs a hearing device. Her discarding of the hearing aid suggests, figuratively, her achievement of independence. This ability to function on her own is represented in the text in various ways. For instance, as she sets out in her search for the source of the laugh, she rejects the policeman's offer of help. Lawrence tells us, "She did not lean at all on the support of the big hand" ("The Last Laugh" 634).[40] Later, when she sees Marchbanks follow the young woman into her house, she takes off her hearing aid and "seem[s] to stretch herself, to stretch her limbs free" (637). Discarding her previous "inert" look, she tells the policeman of her decision not to wait for Marchbanks. Having decided to continue on her way, James feels a moment of "blithe, unaccustomed sense of power" (637). Not only can she now hear voices that say, "He is here! He's come back!" (638), but she can finally hear the laugh coming from the church. Having heard the laugh, she has arrived home ("I'm home now" 640) in more ways than one. Her new-found independence is reflected in her permission to the policeman to stay and warm himself before he leaves. "You can make up the fire in the sitting-room, and you can go when you are warm," she tells him (640). But since she's otherwise alone, she orders him not to come upstairs (640). It is not until next morning that she can truly appreciate that she can now hear. This new ability to hear and see Pan (the previous night) leads to a new vision of the world. As she looks out of her window, it appears to James that the world of shattered churches that she had seen before is now replaced by another world where the "air all seem[s] rare and different" (641). In this different world, it seems to James "as if some skin or integument ha[s] broken, as if the old, mouldering London sky ha[s] crackled and rolled back, like an old skin, shrivelled, leaving an absolutely new blue heaven" (641). Looking out at this panorama, she realizes that she has been "independent" of Marchbanks all along. For though they have been friends, they have not been lovers. She also realizes that just as she dislikes dogs, she dislikes men because they are so "doggy" (643). Her independence is complete at the end when she stands in her sitting room, separate from the policeman, who was merely "incidental" to her, and from Marchbanks, who was always only a friend, never a lover.

The action, focalized through James, suggests not only her increasing ability to be independent but also her victory over the universe. This idea is reinforced when she is compared to a "nymph." Lawrence evokes a parallel between her and the natural order of the universe. "She had an odd nymph-like inquisitiveness, sometimes like a bird, sometimes a squirrel, sometimes a rabbit: never quite like a woman" (631). By evoking this parallel, Lawrence appears to suggest James's ability to commune with nature and her fellow beings. And since the laugh that James hears is associated with the male principle in Lawrencean myth, her ability to hear this laugh suggests also her ability to succeed in heterosexual relationships. Moreover, since Lawrence validated the heterosexual relation, James's ability to hear the laugh appears to suggest his validation of her as well.

To the feminist, however, the relation between James and a bird, a squirrel, or a rabbit suggests more than her closeness to nature. Through association with littleness and ineffectiveness within the animal kingdom, these terms also suggest Lawrence's belittlement of James. That belittlement comes from that history of sexism in English discussed by Cheris Kramarae and Julia Penelope, among others. Words have power to wound women because of the sexist origins of the English language. For instance, when Lawrence equates women with birds, it wounds them because it reveals a sexist attempt to control women's thinking. By using such metaphors for James, therefore, Lawrence actually suggests her defeat, not her victory.

Further, by cloaking James's defeat beneath a spurious victory, the story deviously presents her as a victim. For like Emmie's helpless and fruitless independence in "You Touched Me," James's independence in "The Last Laugh" is also gained at a price. The narrative, consequently, suggests that her victory in life is a lesser victory than Marchbanks's in death. From the beginning, the text makes our impression of Marchbanks grander by associating him with both Pan and Christ. Because he is described as a "satyr" (630), for instance, his "neighing laugh" and "goat-like eyes" conjure associations with Pan

(632). But Marchbanks is also associated with Christ. Though "his hooked nose" makes him look "like a satanic young priest," the "beautiful lines" on his face make him look "like a faun" with "a doubtful martyred expression. A sort of faun on the cross" (631). In these images, Marchbanks is thus associated with Christ. Described both as a masculine predator (he is also associated with the wolf [634]) and feminine martyr, he assumes an androgynous role. Androgyny, however, is not an idea that Lawrence explores very fully till he writes *The Escaped Cock*. But though Lawrence does not exploit the concept of androgyny in this story, he does present in Marchbanks a male who is victorious even in his death. Consequently, Marchbanks is not an example of a "weak, failed male" as Harris avers (175). Rather, he is a victor whose victory is partly determined by the way in which Lawrence regards Marchbanks's experiences with the Jewess as a martyrdom, but simply regards James's response to experiences with the policeman and Marchbanks as sexual distaste (Lawrence represents James's experience in figures of speech as "mess" ["The Last Laugh" 643]).[41] Though the Jewess has seemed "incidental" to Marchbanks, her incidence is posited as more significant than that of the men with whom James is associated. For instance, the Jewess opens the door to Marchbanks with anticipation and hope that something wonderful may happen. Coyly, and in a "falsely shy voice" (636), she tells Marchbanks that she was waiting for someone to come, a man that she could like. Even in the snow, she is wearing high-heeled shoes to look attractive, and when she beckons, Marchbanks follows her "like a hound" (636). The universe here is very traditionally ordered, with the man as predator and the woman as seductress. The moral is also obvious: both the man and the woman get each other when they follow the rules.

James's encounters, on the other hand, reveal what happens when the untraditional behavior reverses the traditional order of the universe. For example, right from the start, James treats the policeman as an appendage that remains unacknowledged. In contrast to the Jewess, whom Marchbanks may not have known previously, but would know soon (636), James never comes to "know" the policeman. For though he accompanies her on her search for the source of the laugh, she never feels any urgency in his presence, because "he was a decent young man, one of the waiting sort" (637). Even when he follows behind her, all she feels is a desire to laugh at his expense. Feeling "lithe" and "strong," she "could easily run faster than he. If she wished she could easily kill him, even with her hands" (637). Her feeling of triumph is thus accompanied by a thought of murder. Later, when the policeman follows James into her house, she tells him to remain downstairs. She feels no desire to welcome him upstairs in her room, as the Jewess does Marchbanks. In the morning, she is informed by her housekeeper that he is lame. His "lameness" suggests, figuratively, his impotence. Unlike the Jewess, whose open door welcomed Marchbanks with hope and anticipation, James's shut door to a room on the upper floor suggests her lack of desire to "communicate" with him.

James's untraditional behavior is further emphasized in her realization about her relation with Marchbanks. Right from the beginning, because of James's inability to hear the laugh that Marchbanks can hear, there is tension between James and Marchbanks. When Marchbanks leaves James to pursue the Jewess, who he believes is the source of the laugh, James is not pleased. Significantly, it is only when he is gone from her sight that she takes off her hearing aid and takes on a "martial look." The "slightly anxious, bewildered look of her face" is now gone. But though she feels "free" and "sure," this feeling of independence is accompanied by "pride"; what's more, her new-found "surety" is "dangerous" (637). When she tells the policeman that it is no use waiting for Marchbanks, her laugh is "odd" and "brief." Thus, because James's feeling of "triumph" is accompanied by, among others, a feeling of "rosy anger" (637), Lawrence diminishes the significance of her achievement of independence.

This diminishment is once again apparent in the nature of James's realization about her feelings for Marchbanks in particular and men in general. The morning after James hears the laugh, she realizes "the ridiculousness of being in love . . . [,] of chasing a man or being chased by a man" (642). She realizes that she is over thirty and she's never really wanted a man, that she had merely imagined herself to be in love with Marchbanks; therefore, all she has ever experienced is friendship. She feels that men and women chasing after each other (as she has seen Marchbanks and the Jewess do) look "ridiculous," and she's thankful that she has not made such a "humiliating mistake" (642). Unable to understand why her friend disappeared with the woman the night before, she decides that life is incomprehensible and "messy." She also realizes that given the opportunity, her policeman would also be "messy" like a dog. That James is unable to understand what attracted Marchbanks and the Jewess to each other and that she realizes she is not attracted to men herself suggest a dichotomy between her realization about her sexuality and her ability to hear the laugh of Pan—the representative of the male principle. Consequently, her realization undermines her perception of herself as victorious.

Further, since James achieves independence at the expense of the men in her life, the story encourages our belief in Lawrence's essentialist ideas about "cocksure women." Lawrence seems to suggest here not only that women can, but that they certainly do, appropriate the realm of power (a hitherto male enclave). But, by doing so, he suggests they act against their natural instincts. Similarly, any male submission that results from their action also goes against the natural order of human behavior. This confusion of traditional roles leads to unhappiness, especially as women's achievement is presented as a non-achievement. Therefore, despite James's relation to the natural universe, her ability to hear Pan's bacchic laughter, have a vision of him and throw off her hearing device, she is presented as if she has suffered defeat.

James's "defeat" is especially evident when we analyse Lawrence's ironic use of the metaphor of the laugh itself. What does the laugh represent? Since it is elusive, we may speculate that on one level it may represent the ungraspable truth in life, that which exists in its perfect Platonic state, but which is difficult to achieve and adopt. On another level, the laugh may represent the spirit of nature and the need for human beings to find it within themselves, or without, to lead their lives fully. As a result, James, who hears the laugh, survives, while the men who do not hear the laugh become lame or die. Since the laugh is finally heard only by the woman, Lawrence may appear to suggest that the "natural spirit" is something only women can grasp. Were it so, it would suggest an exceptional support of women in Lawrence's canon.

But a closer reading of the text reveals a dichotomy in Lawrence's presentation of the fictional action that bears on that support. Though James appears to assume power by being able to hear the laugh, her power shows to be malignant and is thus undercut by its consequences—the impotence or death of men. Unlike the Jewess, James shuts her door to the men and remains inviolate—but alone—in her room. Though the focus of past criticism on this story is on the consequences of her decision for the men, I believe that the consequences of her decision in relation to the growth of her character are equally significant. The text unmistakeably suggests Lawrence's complicity with patriarchal notions by portraying James's decision to be alone and her lack of desire for a man as unnatural. The text reveals that a woman ends up divided against herself when she undertakes independence. Consequently, her independence is characterized as grotesque. Moreover, because she desires to be touched by the "spirit," and not a real man (643), her desire for the intangible is mocked as "ridiculous." James may *think* she has grasped the spirit of Pan and therefore may perceive herself as victorious, but since the action of the story suggests that she has not incorporated the message of Pan in her life, her victory is gained at great cost. What's worse, the laugh of Pan may also be mocking her because, in the final analysis, despite human endeavor, the "spirit of nature" is not graspable at all. Lawrence thus suggests that human frailty eliminates the possibility of communication with others.

Lawrence experiments in this story by portraying an unmarried female—James—as capable of being as independent as the male. He emphasizes her equality to the male by constantly referring to her by her last name—a stereotypical way of referring to men in culture. Despite the fact that the text appears to focus on the pyrrhic nature of James's victory by emphasizing its negative consequences on both the female and the male, his text does not uphold patriarchy. In fact, the text also reveals the significance of Marchbanks's withdrawal from his search for the source of the laugh of Pan. The text thus creates a parallel between James and Marchbanks: her independence is as illusory and as self-defeating as that of Marchbanks. Lawrence thus designs a text that not merely demonstrates the hollowness of the female's desire to achieve independence from the male but also the hollowness of such a debilitating desire in any human being—female or male. Further, by portraying both females and males as losers in this story, the text reveals a dark and fearful image of a world that lacks any system of social organization because women have left their appointed natural place, the henhouse.

V

Begun in 1926 and published in 1927, "Two Blue Birds" is a story about a husband and wife, Mr. and Mrs. Gee, who know each other so well that they can no longer live together, except once a year. On one of Mrs. Gee's visits to her husband, she finds him settled in splendor with a menage of three women. Miss Wrexall, the twenty-eight-year-old woman who served as Mr. Gee's secretary, had brought in with her two others—her younger sister as valet cum maid and their mother as cook. Miss Wrexall's quiet devotion to Mr. Gee as she listens to him all day, takes notes, and types in triplicate all he says irritates his wife. Therefore, one day, when Mrs. Gee sees two blue birds fighting at her husband's feet as he sits dictating to his secretary in the garden, she sees a similarity between the birds and Miss Wrexall and herself. Consequently, she joins her husband and invites Miss Wrexall to tea. This meeting between the wife and the secretary is confrontational. While Mrs. Gee accuses the secretary of cheapness because she is too giving to her employer, the secretary considers herself not cheap precisely because she's so giving. Since Miss Wrexall is unable, or refuses, to comprehend Mrs. Gee's point of view, Mrs. Gee withdraws from this confrontation having decided not to be like the blue birds: she will not fight for the possession of her husband.

Because much of the criticism surrounding this story focuses on the marital relation between Mr. and Mrs. Gee and on the centrality of the male to the two females (his wife and secretary), it obscures the significance of Miss Wrexall and her relation with Mrs. Gee. Indeed, the final scene of confrontation between the wife and the secretary, with Mr. Gee in the middle, epitomizes the triangular relation between the husband, the wife, and the secretary. Kingsley Widmer, among other critics, views this confrontation as unnecesssary and totally lifeless, for he senses conflict and strife in the two fighting blue birds, not an assertion of pulsating life. He opines that

> [i]nstead of fighting like one of the real blue birds, the wife gives up her husband to the vulgar and devoted little secretary. As for herself, she is too intelligent to allow any man to have "two blue birds of happiness to flutter around his feet, tearing out their little feathers." (109)

Widmer interprets the entire sequence as sterile, because, to him, the wife's "willful and intelligent self-consciousness" appears to be similar to that of "the whole mode of the fiction itself" (109-10). Consequently, he finds Mrs. Gee's confrontation perverse.

"Two Blue Birds," however, is not merely a story about a marriage relation gone sour; it is also a story about the lack of sisterhood among women. Harris, therefore, correctly reads the confrontation between Mrs. Gee and Miss Wrexall as constructive. She asserts that by pointing out Miss Wrexall's self-sacrifice and the parasitical nature of her relation with Mr. Gee, Mrs. Gee breaks "up a relationship that has been bleeding her husband of whatever literary abilities he might have and his secretary of any sense of her own value as a woman and an independent human being" (208).[42] But their exchange at the end leads to an impasse because of Miss Wrexall's refusal to affirm as natural the authority of Mrs. Gee's speech. By marginalizing the significance of Mrs. Gee's speech, Miss Wrexall perpetuates patriarchal attitudes toward women's speech. Among other things, feminists have advocated a matriarchal bond or sisterhood among women as a means of countering patriarchal attitudes. Adrienne Rich is one of the foremost proponents of this idea. What she says about lying with regard to relationships among women is significant to our understanding of the constitution of the female self:

> The liar may resist confrontation, denying that she lied. Or she may use other language: forgetfulness, privacy, the protection of someone else. Or, she may bravely declare herself a coward. This allows her to go on lying, since that is what cowards do. . . .
>
> Truthfulnesss, honor, is not something which springs ablaze of itself; it has to be created between people. . . . (192-194)[43]

In this passage Rich emphasizes the need for truth among women. For truth, no matter how frightening, expands the boundaries of understanding of the self as well as of the other. Examined within the frame Rich provides, the final confrontation between Miss Wrexall and Mrs. Gee demonstrates the lack of "truth" in Miss Wrexall's perception of herself. For, by refusing to see, and to admit, to the heirarchical and binary nature of her relationship with Mr. Gee, Miss Wrexall refuses to confront herself and becomes a "liar" to herself. She thus denies herself the possibility of life. Moreover, by not confronting the truth in Mrs. Gee's argument, by refusing to see anything wrong in slaving for and adoring her employer while he dictates to her, Miss Wrexall continues the old status quo ("Two Blue Birds" 513) and "wrecks all" within, and around, her.

But though Miss Wrexall is unwilling to confront the reality of her relation with her employer, her status as victim is also determined by the influence of her low economic background (518). It is therefore unsurprising that she refuses to question her relation with Mr. Gee (she accepts Mr. Gee's assumption of his superiority as natural) and jeopardize not one but three incomes in her family.

Mr. Gee's captivation and enthrallment of Miss Wrexall with the power of his speech is especially significant because of the ability of language, historically, to create meaning and to impose structure. Briefly, if the mouth is the center or source of power, and words are a means to impose structure, then, in linguistic terms, Cameron Gee, as a writer, constantly dictating notes to his secretary, is empowered by his speech. The story suggests a further interesting parallel between Mr. Gee's choice of topic, the structure of the novel, and his efforts to create structure in his life by employing three women to run his household, for his "men-servants were likely to swindle him" (513), while distancing himself from his wife, who questions his authority. With his domestic life in order, he is "perfectly comfortable" (517). But Mr. Gee's empowerment through language and through the women at his command highlights its lack in Miss Wrexall. Her lesser position as mute devotee is apparent in her silent ingestion of his words and later regurgitation of them in triplicate. Not only does Miss Wrexall not question his speech, but she accepts it with pleasure. In turn, Mr. Gee complacently accepts her acceptance of his needs as natural (513). When he speaks in a "confident voice" with the certainty of knowledge that he'll be "gladly fulfilled," Miss Wrexall, like "all his servants" (513), "adore[s] him" (513). Thus, Mr. Gee's endless dictation to his secretary, despite Mrs. Gee's conviction that he's never kissed Miss Wrexall (518), suggests, figuratively, an act of "sexual" domination.

A silent presence in the background, the younger Miss Wrexall provides Mr. Gee with domestic content and completes his creation of a perfectly balanced picture of his life. He is like a "cock of his own walk, made much of by his own hens" (517). He creates this picture of domestic bliss by accepting the Wrexalls' services and economies on his behalf as natural (513). Their economies are reminiscent of Miss Frost's and Miss Pinnegar's attitude toward James Houghton's affairs in *The Lost Girl,* where "when a creditor became dangerous" the secretary "*always* smoothed over the financial crisis" (516). Such concern for an employer, however, is beyond the call of duty. On the one hand, the sisters' efforts to overcome their economic necessity through employment are laudatory; on the other hand, their excessive self-abnegation is demeaning to their character. In this regard, Harris correctly notes that Mrs. Gee is

> revolted by the ways Gee uses these three women, by the pleasure they get out of being used, and by the complacency that has crept into his writing. Her credo on human relationships is . . . "His comfortableness didn't consist so much in good food or a soft bed, as in having nobody and nothing to contradict him. 'I do like to think he's got nothing to aggravate him,' the secretary had said to the wife. 'Nothing to aggravate him!' What a position for a man! Fostered by women who would let nothing aggravate him". (207)

Within such convenient circumstances, it is conceivable that Miss Wrexall shall continue to serve Mr. Gee, content to live meagerly herself by convincing herself that in doing so she was not selling herself short.

Lawrence further emphasizes the significance of language in this story by evoking Biblical associations of the Creation to draw a parallel with the relation between Miss Wrexall and Mr. Gee. Biblical associations between language and the "word" of God conjure and uphold the cultural associations of godliness with the control of language. For instance, "[i]n the silence of midnight" Mrs. Gee heard Mr. Gee's "voice in the distance, dictating away, like the voice of God to Samuel" ("Two Blue Birds" 518). Further, by using the word "adore" to describe the secretary's attitude toward Mr. Gee, Lawrence sets up a hierarchy between the two. The secretary obviously looks up to Mr. Gee and to his words. Her attitude creates a feudal structure between her and him. Further, the language of feudal stratification defines their relation and emphasizes the significance of his position in her life. Miss Wrexall's attitude toward Mr. Gee evokes that *status quo* between the "self" and the "other" which defines all relationships. To some feminists that status quo defines the relation of the female self to a patriarchal society. For example, French feminists adopt psychoanalysis, and especially Lacan, as a means to understand this status quo. In Lacanian terms, therefore, Mr. Gee functions as the "Other" to Miss Wrexall, and she constitutes her personality in relation to him. Mrs. Gee understands this, but not Miss Wrexall, who tries to re-assure Mrs. Gee at the end that her "giving" reflects her strength, not her undervaluing herself (527).

By describing Miss Wrexall's behavior as too giving, as well as by associating the Wrexall family with performing "the miracle of loaves and fishes daily" (516), Lawrence once again introduces and subverts the Christ principle in this story. Lawrence's views on Christ and Christianity are well documented. For instance, in a letter to Catherine Carswell in 1916 Lawrence had written that

> Christianity is based on reaction, on negation really. It says, "Renounce all worldly desires, and live for heaven." Whereas I think people ought to fulfil sacredly their desires. And this means fulfilling the deepest desire to live unhampered by things. . . . The Christian was hampered by property, because he must renounce it. And to renounce a thing is to be subject to it. Reaction against any force is the complement of that force. So Christianity is based too much on reaction. . . .
>
> But I count Christianity as one of the great historical factors, the has-been. That is why I am not a conscientious objector: I am not a Christian. . . . I too believe man must fight.
>
> But because a thing *has been*, therefore I will not fight for it. Because . . . a man's property is symbol for his manhood, I will not fight for the symbol. Because this is *a falling back*. . . . And we must break through the film which encloses us one with the past, and come out into the new. (*Collected Letters* I 465-66)

Together with Lawrence's philosophical attitude toward Christianity and the characterization of Mrs. Gee and Miss Wrexall, Lawrence's text thus appears to contrast the two opposing principles of "give" and "take." Too much giving, which is traditionally associated with Christ's love for humankind (this theme is especially well developed in *The Escaped Cock*), as well as with female submission, is therefore posited as unhealthy. In Christian terms, this opinion has long been regarded as blasphemy. More generally, this attitude seems to suggest that far from touting the politics of male domination and female submission, Lawrence was, in fact, stating that women must be less submissive than they have traditonally been known to be. Such an interpretation is in keeping with Lawrence's statement to Blanche Jennings: "I prefer a little devil—a Carmen—I like nothing passive" (*Collected Letters* I 44), and his self-professed views on fighting for the women's cause. What renders these views suspect, however, is that they are propagated through the means of a character, Mrs. Gee, whose independence of spirit is presented in predatory terms.

As opposed to Miss Wrexall, Mrs. Gee dislikes her husband's words and kisses. She empowers herself by discovering her own language.[44] Feminists such as Luce Irigaray, Helene Cixous, Julia Kristeva, and others, propose that the mouth suggests the figurative mouth of the vagina—the center of female power.[45] If we accept their figuration to understand Lawrence's text, Mrs. Gee's desire to express herself sexually as well as through speech suggests her assumption of power over language. Her subsequent sexual independence and constant linguistic challenge to her husband and later to his secretary rips the veil of her husband's illusory position of authority—a position that he has assumed in relation to all the women in his employ. Her empowerment through speech is her means of achieving her "difference." Her new-found independence, however, is mitigated by being framed as wolf-like or "devouring."[46] This association evokes a parallel between Mrs. Gee and Winifred in "The Witch a la Mode." As in that story, we question here such a designation. From a feminist perspective we understand that the negative association between Mrs. Gee's linguistic challenge to her husband and predatoriness is age-old. Outspokenness in women in history has been stereotyped as a devouring act. Adrienne Rich, in *On Lies, Secrets, and Silence*, discusses the silence surrounding the history of feminist literary tradition:

> Yet still a Mary Wollstonecraft (labelled "the hyena in petticoats") is viewed without reference to her forbears, not only the sixteenth-century women pamphleteers but the wisewomen and witches, who had been the objects of wholesale persecution and massacre for three centuries. (11)

Because Mrs. Gee is aware that her husband's power and pride lie in his words, she wounds his pride with her insult that his books read as if "Miss Wrexall had written them from . . . [his] hints" ("Two Blue Birds" 526). Like Winifred's speech, in "The Witch a la Mode," that represents a threat to Coutts and that he "overthrows" by returning to his fiancee, Mrs. Gee's linguistic challenge, too, represents a threat to Mr. Gee's authority that he "overthrows" by accepting as natural the adoration of an unquestioning secretary.

Just as Mrs. Gee's acquisition of speech is presented negatively, so is her sexual liberation denigrated for being inappropriate and insincere. The text thus reveals here Lawrence's complicity in patriarchal misogyny. For instance, as she is not ready to "turn into a pillar of salt," Mr. Gee advises her to "make pickled cucumber of them [the men], before you crystallize out" (514). Mrs. Gee wonders whether he means "to suggest that he himself ha[s] been well pickled and that further immersion . . . [is] for him unnecessary" (514). Since her obvious infidelities are "part of her modern necessity" (514), Mr. Gee can only impose his sarcasm on her. But Mr. Gee's "catty" remarks (514) introduce the possibility that her "predatory" instincts may be the result of her sexual dissatisfaction with her husband. Lawrence, however, complicates interpretation by suggesting that Mrs. Gee's infidelities do not necessarily indicate her boredom with her husband. In her thoughts, not only does she refer to the secretary as a "young girl,"[47] but she also focuses on her own age. She is in her fortieth year. Further, the spring in the air and the garden surroundings within which she finds her husband dictating to his secretary make her unsure whether she wants to be kissed by her husband or not (518). All these factors contribute in undermining her "advice" to Miss Wrexall. Finally, her anger at a patriarchal system wherein the male (her husband) is happy to take and the female (the secretary) is happy to give is ultimately fruitless. She realizes that within such a system there is no place for a woman like her who questions patriarchal authority. This realization in her signifies her defeat and merely illustrates Lawrence's ideas about "cocksure women" who appropriate traditionally male roles and are more cocky than the men themselves. Appropriately, then, their cockiness is regarded as unnatural and unfruitful (555).

Lawrence's apparent chauvinism is reinforced by the fact that not only does he minimize the impact of Mrs. Gee's speech by figuratively describing it as devouring, but by adopting the metaphor of two fighting birds to describe the final confrontation between the wife and the secretary he figuratively compares their speech to that of a bird. He thus perpetuates the streotypical presentations of women speakers as "*shrews, bitches, cats, hens; shrill, sharp-tongued, and gossipy*" (Kramarae xiii). Further, by comparing both women to birds, Lawrence suggests that Mrs. Gee's independence is equivalent to Miss Wrexall's silence toward Mr. Gee. Since Mr. Gee considers the Wrexall menage as part of his hen-coop, by equating his wife to Miss Wrexall he is able to extend his menage.

Finally, though this story may be read in alternative ways, Lawrence allows the victory of the male perspective over the female perspective. For instance, Mr.

Gee dictates to his secretary that "[i]n every novel there must be one outstanding character . . . with whom we always sympathise . . . even when we are most aware of the human frailties" (521). His dictation to his secretary suggests that in the story of his life, he is the character with whom he sympathizes most. Just like Mr. Gee's, Mrs Gee's ability to stand up for herself suggests her equivalent selfishness. But when her "selfish" reading of life conflicts with that of her husband, Mr. Gee emerges as victorious. Mr. Gee implements his victory both by his silence when his wife and secretary fight over him and by speaking only when no one contradicts him, such as with his female help. Reading against the grain, the text reveals that Mr. Gee uses speech and silence in strategic ways to insure his victory. On the one hand, knowing that his speech shall remain unchallenged by his female help, he empowers himself over them by his speech. On the other hand, unable to respond to the challenge in his wife's speech, he mostly remains silent in her presence. Thus, though the text shows how Mr. Gee dominates the women in his life, it does not uphold his means to success. By showing Mr. Gee's need and ability to adopt such manipulative strategies to empower himself over his financial dependents, the text, in fact, reveals the weakness of a patriarchy that so inflates itself.

Lawrence wrote this story very late in his career at a time when he had begun to create women more agreeable to feminist views, yet, in many ways, it appears merely to perpetuate an image of inferiority in women. But though he portrays Miss Wrexall as a mostly silent figure in this story, by showing how Mr. Gee, a male author—successfully—"writes" the lives of his female "help," Lawrence demonstrates the impact of the patriarchy on unmarried females when they occupy an economically subservient position.

***

Despite the fact that the narrative mode of the short stories discussed above often presents both the female and the male characters as the focalizer whose perceptions influence interpretation of the texts, the texts do not encourage us to adopt a gynocentric perspective. My gynocentric approach to these stories often shows what otherwise may have remained hidden, and what Lawrence may not have at all seen, either. Since past critics overlook the significance of unmarried female characters such as Winifred, Emma, Emmie, Miss James, and Miss

Wrexall in the interests of studies on male characters or the marriage relation, my chapter has been an attempt to uncover the significance of these female characters by giving them a voice, and, in effect, an existence in history. Further, my study demonstrates Lawrence's ambivalence toward women and women's issues. Though Lawrence's portrayal of unmarried females often depicts them as victims of patriarchy, his portrayal is nonetheless qualified by the text as it reveals how insidiously the patriarchy carries out its victimization. Though the text often reveals Lawrence's complicity with the patriarchy, it reveals, at other times, his effort to critique the patriarchy. Lawrence's *oeuvre*, thus, both shows unmarried women as victims of the patriarchy and exposes a weakness in the patriarchy that can perpetuate its power only through suppression and bullying of others.

Chapter 3

The Short Stories: Part II

Rather than focus on the older unmarried female characters as I did in the previous chapter, in this one I will focus on their younger counterparts. The young unmarried female characters I focus on are the anonymous female and Elaine in "The Primrose Path," Annie and the female tram attendants in "Tickets, Please," Miss Stokes in "Monkey Nuts," and Elsa in "The Overtone."[48] My study of these characters demonstrates that Lawrence differentiates between them and their older counterparts on the basis of their sexuality and their economic status. While he presents the older female characters as, primarily, sexually inexperienced, he presents the younger female characters as sexually experienced. Such presentation depicts agist attitudes and androcentric fulfillment of male desire. The male does not value the older female sexually so doesn't cast her in those terms, while the younger female is cast differently. Further, since the younger female characters represent a lower economic group, Lawrence seems to suggest that sexual freedom is more common among people less bound to status and hence one's image in the eye of the other. (This idea is common in much of Lawrence's fiction such as *Lady Chatterley's Lover*.) But though the younger female characters are more assertive in their acts and utterances, Lawrence portrays them all as silenced under patriarchal law.

As with the older unmarried characters, so with the younger ones Lawrence makes use of specific images from culture to enrich his fictional representation. For instance, in "The Primrose Path," Lawrence evokes the image of the prostitute through his representation of an anonymous young female and Elaine. But though both of them assert themselves by demanding material assets for their sexual favors, they are devalued by a society that refuses even to acknowledge their existence. Annie and the other female tram attendants, in "Tickets, Please," represent urban lower-class working women. They assert themselves when they corner the local casanova, John Raynor, and force him to choose one of them to marry. But because the action suggests their dissatisfaction with their revenge, their assertive act is undone. Miss Stokes, in "Monkey Nuts," represents the rural working-class. In this story, she asserts herself when she willfully pursues Joe, but she stands defeated and humiliated when her pursuit is ridiculed by Joe's male peers in his army unit. Finally, in "The Overtone,"[49] Elsa Laskell tells Mr. Renshaw of her decision to be more assertive in her relations with men, but her decision is undermined by the fact that she espouses the cause of the heterosexual relation. My study of the younger unmarried female characters therefore suggests that Lawrence's images of unmarried women from contemporary life portray women who participate in increasingly assertive acts. Lawrence experiments in his presentation of unmarried women by granting the younger females a sexual existence that is untinged by the ambiguity of presentation that marks stories such as "The Christening."[50] He also portrays them with a voice. Though his experimentation appears to challenge patriarchy, his images of these females also diminish their character because they portray them as ruthless, hurtful, and selfish, asserting once again the allegiance of Lawrence's imagination to essentialist definitions of women.

I

"The Primrose Path," written in 1913, focuses on a young man, Daniel Berry, who is visiting his maternal uncle, Daniel Sutton. During this visit, Berry learns about his uncle' relations with women. He is aware that Sutton married at the age of eighteen and had two daughters, but because of differences in disposition from that of his wife, he was unhappy in his relations with her. "He [i]s a blustering, impetuous man, she [i]s rather cold in her soul, d[oes] not care about anything very much, [and i]s rather capable and close with money"(429). Sutton tells his nephew that because he felt circumscribed by his wife's cold nature, he immigrated to Australia with a young woman (whose name we are not told), who, however, soon left him for another man. Suspecting her of trying to murder him, Sutton returned to England, but since his wife (who is now living with another man) refused to take him back, he set up residence with Elaine, a young woman of twenty-one from a lower-class impoverished background. Hearing about Elaine makes Berry feel indignant on behalf of his now dying aunt, but when Sutton, who is adamant about marrying Elaine, offers to introduce Berry to her, Berry accepts. At Elaine's house, seeing the manner in which she is able to manipulate Sutton's affections despite his gruff behavior with her, Berry predicts that she will eventually leave him. The final line of this story abruptly informs us that his predictions come true.

This story has not motivated much criticism. While Emile Delavenay (157-58) and Harry T. Moore (23) approach the story in biographical terms, Graham Hough dismisses it as a story that falls short of what it promises to deliver (173), and Kingsley Widmer interprets it in terms of a dialectic between "sensuality and terror" in the uncle's world (25). In all cases, the female characters are left out of the count.

As opposed to previous critics, I believe that the peripheral significance that Sutton and the story accord to the women in Sutton's life perpetuates patriarchal attitudes toward them. From the beginning, each time Sutton fails in his relations with them, he blames it on them. For example, though he, himself, is rather coarse in his speech, he notices his wife's "common accent." Because "that cold twang in her voice torture[s] him with shame[,] . . . he stamp[s] down in bullying and in becoming more violent in his own speech" (429). By finding fault with his wife, Sutton refuses to recognize his own shortcomings and transfers responsibility from himself to her for the failure of their relation. Indeed, soon after they marry, he blames his wife for giving away one of their children, refusing to recognize that he has "an emotional man's fear of sentiment, which help[s] to nip his wife from putting out any shoots" (430). Berry, too, recalls that his mother, who is Sutton's older sister, thought he had grown into a bully (429). Moreover, we are informed that his wife truly loves him, but "[w]ith a chaos of a man such as he, she ha[s] no chance of being anything but cold and hard" (430).

The omniscient narrator of this story thus lays the foundation for Sutton's willful movement away from his wife and toward the other female characters.

But by emphasizing the discontent that marks the end of Sutton's relation with his wife, the narrator also prepares us for Sutton's attitude toward the later characters. For example, disregarding his own deficiencies, Sutton leaves his wife to establish "a new menage" with a "sentimental young woman who read[s] Browning" (430). But soon, feeling threatened, Sutton abandons her and goes away to another city where he gets better in no time at all (431). Sutton informs his nephew that he feared that this "devil" was trying to poison him to be rid of him, and to get "in with another fellow" (431). Significantly, this young female with whom Sutton immigrates to Australia does not have a name. Her anonymity, however, both marginalizes and universalizes her character. On the one hand, her anonymity correlates with her brief presence in Sutton's life and suggests her dramatic insignificance. On the other hand, it suggests the constant "use" to which Sutton puts young females: first the unnamed female and then Elaine. Since the narrative mode of this story allows us to hear of this relation only through Sutton, she remains a voiceless shadow from his past. Therefore, when Sutton tells his version of the story to Berry, not only does he impose his voice over hers, but he also makes her invisible and denies her an identity, a center from which to speak, by keeping her nameless. Further, he successfully vilifies her by associating her behavior with that of the devil and by accusing her of trying to murder him. "That other devil tried to poison me," he tells Berry (431). Hearing his uncle vilifying this unknown female character, Berry correctly interprets it as an expression of Sutton's "fear of life, of death, of himself" (431).

But Sutton's vilification of the anonymous young female represents more than his individual fear; it represents the history of such patriarchal fear which has often resulted in hysterical mud slinging, character bashing, and cruelty toward women. Threatened by assertive women, the patriarchs in the past often maligned women for being devils, or witches, and ostracized them from society and burned them at the stake.[51] In this story, Lawrence evokes, in fact, the female fiend, a character found in nineteenth-century fiction that is similar to the tradition of women burned as witches during the Renaissance. Joseph Andriano's study of the female fiend in nineteenth-century fiction by male writers shows how this fictional device unmasks not only men's attitude toward their art and toward the women in their lives, but also toward their own femininity. His study demonstrates the "breakdown of boundaries between masculine self and feminine 'other' . . . [to] better comprehend the psychodynamics of the male ego in action" (8). Andriano believes that "[t]he phenomenology of the female demon reveals that she is a persistent symbol of our two most impelling instincts, the erotic and the thanatotic [sic]. . . . The haunted man's 'sacred terror' . . . is a sign of her bipolarity: she is both feared and loved" (3). Framed in Andriano's terminology, Lawrence's text of "The Primrose Path" reveals that Sutton, the "haunted man," experiences "sacred terror" when he discovers both his love and fear of the anonymous young female. Under these circumstances, his only recourse is to flee from the cause of fears that outweigh his love.

Sutton replaces the young female in Australia with Elaine in England. In contrast to the anonymous young woman, Elaine is a more clearly realized character. When Sutton meets his nephew, he informs him that he intends to marry her. Later at Elaine's house, seeing his uncle with Elaine, Berry understands how perfectly in control his uncle is. "Already Berry could see that his uncle had bullied them, as he bullied everybody. But they [Elaine and her mother] were used to unpleasant men, and seemed to keep at a distance" ("The Primrose Path" 438). Berry soon realizes, however, that Elaine is not as naive and innocent as Sutton appears to believe. He sees that despite her timidity around his uncle she knows how to humor him. She knows about Maud, Sutton's ailing wife, and is ready to take her in, as well as their daughter, Winnie. Berry also sees that Elaine is fascinated with Sutton and is embarrassed by the way in which she ignores the presence of other people around him. In Sutton's presence, she simpers around him and turns his domination into passion. For example, when Sutton follows Berry into her house, he is in a sullen mood. When he gets up restlessly and walks out of the door, she determinedly follows him out and asks him why he had come. She tries to soothe his temper and get him to relax by coaxing him to take off his coat. At this time, Berry notices that she is

> pale, rather frightened-looking, and . . . her face . . . [i]s drawn slightly with love and fear and misery. . . . She [i]s playing with passion, afraid of it, and really wretched because it le[aves] her, the person, out of count. Yet she continue[s]. (439)

As she coaxes Sutton out of his ill-humor, there comes "into his bearing, into his eyes, the curious smile of passion, pushing away even the death-horror" (439). Seeing the interaction between Sutton and Elaine, Berry realizes that she is more than capable of looking after herself and that his uncle does not really recognize her strength.

Unaware of Elaine's strength, Sutton belittles Elaine. Though Sutton tells Berry that Elaine is a "marvel" (431), he constantly assumes terms for her that emphasize her youth and diminish her character. Briefly, Sutton describes Elaine to Berry as "the best *little woman* in the Midlands . . . a *good girl*—a *beautiful little thing* . . ., [a] *respectable girl*" (my italics 431). By referring to Elaine as the "little woman," a word commonly used to denominate a housewife, Sutton conjures the image of Elaine as less than an adult. By calling her a "girl," he reinforces this image and perpetuates sexist attitudes toward women that the word has carried for centuries. Julia Penelope explains the significance of the term "girle" in relation to old patriarchal attitudes toward women. She asserts that "*girle*, whose etymology is obscure, doesn't appear until the ME period, and then [it appears] as a generic in 1290 that refer[s] to children in general, becoming a [+female] term between 1290 and 1530" (98). Penelope also asserts that by "1530 *girle* referrred only to female children and was commonly applied to all young, **unmarried** women. Its addition indicates increased specificity with respect to the chronological age of individuals, especially females, during the intervening 240 years" (98). By referring to Elaine as a "girl," Sutton emphasizes her youth and—by contrast—his own maturity. He highlights his own mature years again when he pompously refers to her as a "respectable girl" ("The Primrose Path" 431). Since the etymology of the word "girl" carries within itself connotations of being "respectable," or sexually innocent (Penelope 96), Sutton's conversation with Berry reinforces this association and also suggests that because he considers Elaine respectable, he is prepared to reward her with marriage ("The Primrose Path" 431). Finally, Sutton totally dehumanizes Elaine when he calls her "a beautiful little thing" (431). This dehumanization is evident a little later at her house where just as he stoops to fondle his dogs, "paying no attention to them," he abstractedly gazes at her, seeing "something impersonal, the female, not the woman" (438). As Sutton looks down at Elaine, she turns pale, is frightened, and averts her face from him. When she tries to help the "solidly planted" man take off his coat—while he persists in staring straight ahead of him—her face is drawn with "love and fear and misery" (439). Sutton's almost unseeing gaze on Elaine thus demonstrates his power over her, for it objectifies her and robs her of the opportunity to tell her own story.

If Sutton belittles Elaine by objectifying her, she avenges herself when she finally leaves him. Witnessing her strength of will with his uncle, Berry had correctly predicted the end of their relation. But though the final statement about her leaving is dramatically satisfying, it amounts to nothing more than a grand gesture trailing a host of questions. Given her lower class servile background and her poverty, we could speculate that like the woman with whom Sutton went to Australia, Elaine, too, may have merely exchanged one kind of submission for another. For prostitution offers little stability as a profession and none as a social phenomenon.

For various people, prostitution may suggest either the idea of submission or domination. Pierre L. Horn and Mary Beth Pringle, in their introduction to *The Image of the Prostitute in Modern Literature*, trace the various faces of prostitution that both male and female writers have presented. Their study concludes that in contrast to female writers, who humanize their prostitutes, male writers stereotype them by objectifying them. Further expanding on this issue, Diane Bornstein divides the virgin and the prostitute into separate categories, but Nor Hall adopts myth to trace independence as a common trait shared by the two.[52] She asserts that the term "virgin" does not imply chastity, but being true to one's own nature and instinct. The prostitute, on the other hand, also submits "to the demands of [her] instinct, to the chaos of nature" (11). Hall thus concludes that "[t]he prostitute and the virgin are both archetypes or archaic images of the free woman, as opposed to domesticated woman . . . whose life goal is union with the male" (11-12). Hall's definition conjures an image of strength and empowerment.

Though Lawrence evokes in Elaine and the anonymous female images of the archetype of the "free woman," he does not recreate images of strength in them. He objectifies his prostitutes in his story. Briefly, despite the politics of gender and power that prostitution suggests and despite Victorian prudery, Lawrence's story is informed by the fact that changing mores and laws in England had resulted in the legalization and regulation of prostitution in the 1860s. Indeed, the "age of consent [for prostitution] was set at twelve years of age," says Kate

Millett (103).[53] Lawrence emphasizes the relative youth of both the females with whom Sutton is involved. For example, when Berry asks his uncle Elaine's age, Sutton replies, defensively, that she is twenty-one. "Poor thing," says Berry. But for Sutton "*[s]he's* right enough" ("The Primrose Path" 431). Berry also notes her almost boyish figure. He notices "how her skirt hung almost flat on her hips" and that she "was young, scarce developed, a long, slender thing" (437). In addition, her poverty-stricken background, her fear on hearing that Sutton has been visiting his ailing wife, and her eagerness to please Sutton—all demonstrate her servile and financially dependent position in this relationship.

Lawrence certainly complicates the issue by presenting Sutton's behavior through the lens of a silent observer, Berry. Berry's final statement of belief that it would serve Sutton right when Elaine hates him and leaves him raises the question of who is the focalizer of this story: Berry or Sutton? For the answer, we need look no further than Lawrence's presentation of the image of prostitution in his portrayal of the two young females. Like Simone de Beauvoir, I disagree with the association between prostitution and independence. Like Beauvoir, I believe that the independence of prostitutes "is the deceptive obverse of a thousand dependencies . . . [and] this liberty is itself negative" (572). By being financially dependent on Sutton the two females demonstrate that they have not really achieved independence. In fact, both Sutton and Berry refer to their independence in derogatory terms. For instance, in the beginning, Sutton justifies the end of his relation with the anonymous young female to his nephew by claiming that she tried to poison him so that she could go to another man. Significantly, later, Berry uses the same word, "poison," to describe Elaine's future feelings for his uncle. "She'll hate him like poison. . . . Then she'll go off with somebody else," he says ("The Primrose Path" 440). By using the same word, even though one indicates an action and the other an emotion, Lawrence achieves, through dramatic repetition, a certain congruency between both relations. Since poison has the power to kill, the text suggests that in this story the two unmarried females are empowered over Sutton. But because this empowerment suggests a possibility of destructiveness in both females, it is important to question its implications within the text.

In this story, Lawrence challenges patriarchy by evoking an image of prostitution in his portrayal of the two young females. These prostitutes, however, are not presented in the stereotypical role of victims. Just as—stereotypically—men "use" and discard prostitutes, the two females "use" and discard Sutton. But though Sutton's association of their independence with destructive actions and emotions suggests his fear of rather than control over them, Lawrence diminishes their image by portraying them as abusive of their power as any patriarch. So although Lawrence subscribes to patriarchy and finds women who would defy it to be unnatural and cocky and doomed to unhappiness, he nonetheless admits that patriarchy can be abused and abusive. Lawrence's narrative thus shows that a reprehensible act is so regardless of gender.

II

"Tickets, Please," written in 1918 and published in 1919, revolves around the revenge of some female tram conductors on their local casanova and Inspector of trams, John Thomas Raynor. In the beginning, we are told that the Inspector likes to flirt with the female conductors by day and walk with them by night, committing his affections to no one. Once, when Annie, a sassy independent woman, meets him at a fair, they both decide to go out together. But like his previous relationships, this one with Annie comes to an end. When it ends, Annie is furious. Wanting revenge, she plots with his ex-girlfriends. Their moment for revenge arrives when Raynor breaks up with his latest female friend and once again begins to cast his eyes around. At this time, he decides to go out again with Annie, believing that since in the past, he has indicated his lack of interest in being committed to her, he is in no further "danger" from her. He agrees to meet her after work, but when he arrives at the waiting room, he is confronted by all his past girlfriends. Here, they hold him down, beat him, and compel him to choose one of them for his wife, and then further humiliate him by all refusing him. Finally, when all the women decline to have him, Annie sends him on his way.

While critics such as Graham Hough have largely ignored or dismissed this story because they believe that it serves no "serious" purpose, others such as Widmer and Harris only discuss Lawrence's thematic concerns. For instance, Widmer reads this story as a potted version "of the rhythm of usual love—[between] predatory male and possessive female" (139). Widmer's evaluation of this story, however, does not specify whether he is referring to the "rhythm of usual love" in Lawrencean or generic terms. Consequently, it remains unclear to what extent Widmer is asserting his own opinion or merely reiterating Lawrence's presentation of John Raynor's intention to "remain a nocturnal presence" resisting the "possessive female" ("Tickets, Please" 339).[54] Harris, in contrast to Widmer, sees nothing judgmental in Lawrence's portrayal of the women or of John Raynor. Rather, she prefers to see the final conflict in this story as one between two opposing principles, of independence and commitment (139).

While I agree with Harris that this story may be read as a conflict between two opposing principles, I do not agree that Lawrence withholds judgment on the action. I disagree for two reasons. First, Lawrence's works are replete with stridently expressed opinions and a deeply felt worldview, one that continues to challenge critics like Harris herself. And second, because John Raynor is constantly referred to as John Thomas in "Tickets, Please" (which was initially entitled "John Thomas"), his name conjures associations with Mellors, Connie Chatterley's gamekeeper lover in *Lady Chatterley's Lover* (which was initially entitled *The First Lady Chatterley* and then *John Thomas and Lady Jane*). In "Tickets, Please," Lawrence evokes the association between the two male characters in the two fictions when he says that "[t]he inspector's name is John Thomas Raynor—always called John Thomas, except sometimes, in malice, Coddy" (336). The female tram conductors also emphasize this association, especially during their revenge, when they pinion him to the wall, call him "Coddy" and ask him to "[c]hoose [his] girl" (344). Both the names, "John Thomas" and "Coddy," focus on the Inspector's physical endowments that seem to affect his relations with the women. While "Coddy" is a slang reference to the scrotum, "John Thomas" is perhaps a playful reference to Raynor's penis as it is to Mellors's in *Lady Chatterley's Lover*, a book that revolves around a celebration of phallic consciousness rather than mental prowess.

But though the celebration of the phallic—as embodied in Raynor in this story—remained a life-long Lawrencean concern (as is evident in most of his fiction and non-fiction such as the *Fantasia of the Unconscious*), "Tickets, Please" initially appears to be a story that demonstrates the limitations of phallic consciousness. Lawrence appears to achieve this limitation by portraying the female characters in "Tickets, Please" to be just as assertive as the female characters in "The Primrose Path." Their assertive behavior shows their refusal to be ill-treated and demonstrates strength and solidarity among them. But to determine the nature of their self-assertion, we need to determine what motivates their acts. In the beginning, we are told that Annie is overcome by disbelief when Raynor abandons their relationship. Feeling uncertain and unhappy, she weeps "with *fury, indignation, desolation, and misery.* Then she [has] a *spasm of despair*. And then . . . she determine[s] to *have her own back*" (my italics 339). Since she has a "*shrewd* idea" about which girls Raynor has taken out in the past, she decides to contact them. In the beginning, she contacts Nora. She counters Nora's reluctance to join her by "ironically lapsing into [class and gender] dialect" (339), so that the other girl is induced into a state of sisterhood within which she confesses her knowledge. When this happens, Annie openly declares her hostility toward Raynor. "Hasn't he got a face on him! . . . I don't half like his cheek. I could knock him off the foot-board when he comes round at me," she tells Nora (339-40). Annie agrees with Nora that Raynor will get his just rewards one day, but qualifies her assertion with the suggestion that this will occur only if somebody decides to do it. She reminds Nora that she's got as much reason to bring Raynor down as Annie does. And since Nora is as "*vindictive*" as Annie, they both agree upon a plan for revenge (my italics 340). The italicized words emphasize Annie's state of mind when Raynor discontinues seeing her and show that a desire for revenge impels her to solicit other women who have been similarly treated by him.

The motivation for the females' revenge, the fury of their assault on Raynor, and their state of mind during this time determine our reaction to the final denouement. Briefly, from the start, Lawrence portrays the female tram conductors as sexually liberated. But despite their being sexually liberated, the story suggests that for many, the feminine mystique of wife and motherhood remains unachieved.[55] And it is in order to satisfy this feminine mystique that Annie's revenge—as that of the other females—on Raynor requires him to choose one of them to *marry*. One might argue that they do this with the ultimate intention of refusing him and thus forcing him to feel the deep sense of rejection they experienced each time he walked away. But by depicting these characters as unhappy with their revenge, Lawrence shows their failure. For example, when Raynor chooses Annie to marry, she exclaims, "'Me!' . . . with a terrible *bitter* accent . . . [and draws] away from him with strange *disgust* and *bitterness*." But while she refuses to touch him, "her face quiver[s] with a kind of *agony* [and]

. . . she is overcome by *bitter hopelessness*" (my italics 345). Even Annie's cry to them to stop their vindictiveness is painful: "'Shut up, for God's sake!' cried Annie fiercely, as if in torture" (346).[56] Like Annie, though the other females also refuse to have him, they "wait . . . for him to look at [them]" (345).

Though Lawrence's story portrays female characters as assertive and independent when they avenge themselves on Raynor, it also portrays the hollowness of their revenge. The italicized words—bitter, disgust, hopelessness, and torture—demonstrate that the female characters' act of revenge is borne of dismay at not being Raynor's permanent choice. Their vengeful act diminishes their character because it shows how they lose their self-control and attack a person who refuses to marry them. In fact, since frustration and vindictiveness are the key motives for their action, their act assumes connotations of loss rather than victory. Their vengeance suggests their failure for the same reasons as the prostitutes' treatment of Sutton in "The Primrose Path." As in that story, so here too Lawrence shows women as brutal, a trait as reprehensible and unacceptable in women as it is in Raynor. Though Lawrence tries to deflect our attention from their brutality by demonstrating its success and Raynor's defeat, the self-incriminatory circumstances and the vicious intent motivating their act finally condemns these female characters.

Consequently, at the end, as they watch Raynor depart from the waiting room, their final "*mute, stupified* faces" (my italics 346) are faces of rejected and defeated women who would give a lot for circumstances to be otherwise so they could be Raynor's real choice. For finally, even as they all decline to have him, "each one of them wait[s] for him to look at her, hop[ing] he would look at her" (345). In the waiting room, Annie is the only one who does not look at him with hope, but she does not because "something [i]s broken in her" (345). Because her spirit is broken and because she is hurt, when the other females tell the humiliated Raynor to be a man and leave without a grudge, she tells everyone to keep quiet. Further, even though Annie hands over the key to the door of the "waiting" room to let Raynor out, it is evident that she, like the other females, still occupies a position as circumscribed and in a state of "waiting" and silence as they always have. Though Annie and the other females are able to dominate Raynor physically, they are defeated by their inability to conquer their own desires.

A form of muting, their defeat thus is portrayed as different from that of many other female characters in Lawrence's short fiction where they are physically silenced by male presence or speech. Shirley Ardener, in "The Representation of Women in Academic Models," explains the different ways in which muting in women is "embedded in different social spaces" (4). But though Ardener suggests that being muted "does not necessarily mean being purposefully oppressed" (4), in this story there is purposefulness; Raynor deliberately mutes the tram attendants when he dates them and discards them. He also mutes them when, at the end, he maliciously chooses Annie—the one who leads the other women in their revenge against him. By choosing her, he undoes the reason for her anger to make meaningless her revenge and assert his victory. Further, in agreement with Richard Wheeler, I believe that "[b]y isolating Annie, he forces her to see . . . that the travesty of courtship in the waiting room has not destroyed, but simply brutalized, her longing for intimacy" with him (242-43).

"Tickets, Please" is more than a story about the conflict between phallic and mental prowess; it is a story portraying the weakness possible in both types of prowess. Just as Lawrence portrays Raynor's success as a lover with the females and his ability to silence them, so does he portray the process of muting as reversed when the young females corner Raynor in the waiting room to make him realize what he has done to them. He has turned them into viragoes whose anger momentarily silences him. As Annie and the other females pin him down, Annie is tense and has "a terrifying lust in her voice" that seems to demand blood, not sex. "You ought to be *killed*," she says (344). Hearing the murderous intent in her voice, Raynor is struck "dumb." But though his silence reflects neither glory nor defeat and he recovers his speech when he is able to walk away, in this war between the sexes, Lawrence portrays both women and men as losers.

III

Written in 1919, "Monkey Nuts" focuses on the interaction between Miss Stokes, a young woman who drives a wagon, and military men on civilian duty who unload hay from wagons. When Miss Stokes is attracted to Joe, who is twenty-three years old, she sends him a note asking him to meet her. But under the influence of his forty-year-old corporal, Albert, Joe is too self-conscious to respond independently to Miss Stokes. Despite Albert's mocking her "summons" (369), she remains decisive about wanting to see Joe and asserts herself initially by holding his hand and later by putting her arm around his waist. Joe, however, merely feels mortified by her forwardness, so that the next time she summons him, he submits to Albert's decision to meet her in his stead. But Miss Stokes is offended by Albert's attempts to flirt and walks away from him in tears. The next day when she meets the unit, she confronts Joe and asks him why he did not meet her. But when Joe answers merely by calling her "monkey-nuts," Miss Stokes feels humiliated and leaves amidst the men's laughter.

Previous critics such as Delavenay, Hough, and Tedlock dismiss this tale out of hand, for they see no Lawrencean philosophy behind it, only a presentation of wartime experience. Harris, however, sees a relation between this tale and "Wintry Peacock," both of which in her view show men's separateness from women and their reluctance to follow them. Harris explains that Lawrence emphasizes the men's reluctance by portraying Miss Stokes—despite her assertiveness—as lacking in sense. Thus when she makes a bid for power and for leadership between the sexes, "her voice is shrill, her demand disparaged" (153). Harris says that Lawrence portrays the derogatory association between Miss Stokes's assertiveness and its impact on the men by means of Joe's mockery of her name at the end. By calling her "monkey-nuts," Joe evokes the association of this term with the "slang for coconuts." And since "monkey" can also mean "woman" and "mock," Harris suggests that Joe mocks her attraction for him (153).

Like Harris, I believe that Miss Stokes's behavior is mocked by the all-male unit. But I also believe that when the males in the unit laugh at her attempt to appropriate a traditionally male prerogative, they do not understand the implications of their mockery on themselves. Their laughter reveals their views about Miss Stokes's assertiveness with Joe. By presenting the unit's views regarding Miss Stokes's initiative, Lawrence appears to uphold his views about "cocksure" women. In his essay "Cocksure Women and Hensure Men," Lawrence explains that cocksureness in a woman is both unnatural and unfulfilling. He believes that to be a cocksure woman "is the tragedy of the modern woman" because "she is a hen all the time" (555). For him, cocksureness in a woman

> is all an attitude, and one day the attitude will . . . collapse . . . [and the woman will realize that] she has lost her life. The lovely henny surety, the hensureness which is the real bliss of every female, has been denied her; she had never had it. Having lived her life with such utmost strenuousness and cocksureness, she has missed her life altogether. Nothingness! (555)

The diction of "Monkey Nuts" constructs Miss Stokes as a cocksure woman. Attracted to Joe's "quiet, tender-looking form, young and fresh," she acknowledges to herself that she likes him (368). But since Joe is a "shy bird" (368) and retiring in contrast to the talkative Albert, she must conduct a conversation with Albert while maintaining her "magnetic attention" on Joe. When her gaze fails to elicit the appropriate response from Joe, she sends him a telegram signed M.S. When Joe receives her missive, his "heart melt[s]" and he feels confused and "weak[,] as if he had had a blow" (368). Because Miss Stokes's "summons" (369) arouses such feelings of weakness in Joe, they suggest her power over him. Lawrence also suggests her power in Joe's response to Miss Stokes's reaching out to hold his hand on the road; he feels "staggered" and "mortified" by her behavior (372). Later, when she puts her arm lightly around his waist, he withdraws into silence (373). Lawrence especially emphasizes her power through her name. Though she explains to the males in the unit that her initials, M.S., stand for "monkey-nuts," they would understand this term to be a slang reference to male genitals.[57] By appropriating this term, not only does Miss Stokes empower herself over Joe in traditional terms, but she also pre-empts the typical male response to her attitude.

Though Lawrence portrays Miss Stokes's attempt to step beyond her gender boundaries, he does not portray it as a success. Condemnation of Miss Stokes's assertiveness is evident in the use of the word "monkey" in relation to her. In keeping with Lawrencean paradigms such as his use of animal imagery to delineate character,[58] this story's characterization of Joe and his derogatory association of Miss Stokes with a lower primate known to mimic human action suggests that he views her behavior as undignified and merely an "aping" of male action. Further, like "The Witch a la Mode," "Monkey Nuts" illustrates the power of language to create and impose meaning. By calling Miss Stokes "monkey-nuts" in a mocking fashion, Joe empowers himself with speech and ascribes his meaning to this term. By re-defining it, he successfully silences Miss Stokes. His attitude toward her parallels similar attitudes by the patriarchy toward women. Linguistic studies show that men often use mockery to belittle women and to empty their speech of meaning and importance. For example, Barrie Thorne, Cheris Kramarae, and Nancy Henley, in "Language, Gender and Society: Opening a Second Decade of Research," explain that "labeling of women as parts of body, fruit, or animals and as mindless, or like children—labels with no real parallel for men—reflects men's derision of women and helps maintain gender hierarchy and control" (9). But not only does Joe empower himself with words, he also empowers himself with action. While he does not consider his own efforts to control their relation as inappropriate, he is impatient with her for controlling their relation. For example, when he spies her at the circus, he pretends not to see her. But when she pretends not to see him, it is "a blow to him, and it ma[kes] him angry" ("Monkey Nuts" 371).

Not only does Joe have double standards about how he and Miss Stokes should behave under similar circumstances, he needs support to maintain his position. This male need for a comrade reveals weakness and fear in him. Widmer correctly condemns the male comraderie in this story found during the three-way confrontation between Miss Stokes, Joe, and Albert. Here, he says, "the masculinity of the soldier pals has won its revenge, not only on the female, but on their own sexual longings" (137). The males bond with each other to overcome the impact of Miss Stokes on them. While their victory over her is thus assured, their need to bond at this time reveals their inability to counteract her impact singly and thus suggests the power of her impact. Lawrence demonstrates her power by creating a counterpoint in the two movements between Miss Stokes and Albert when they, alternatively, place their hands on Joe to claim him. In the first movement, just as Winifred in "The Witch a la Mode" raises her arms thrice toward Coutts to hold him back with her but is unsuccessful, so does Miss Stokes call out thrice to Joe, but is unable to make him follow her lead. When Miss Stokes puts her hands on Joe, he is "mortified" ("Monkey Nuts" 372) and is unable to speak. He feels "maddened, but helpless" (373), and so there is total silence between them. Here, despite her physical effort, Miss Stokes fails to make Joe respond to her. In fact, Joe feels silenced by Miss Stokes's assertiveness and tries to gain the upper hand by silencing her in his turn by calling her "monkey-nuts." His mockery of her looks forward to his later relief at being rid of Miss Stokes's attentions—a relief that is greater than his reaction to the cease-fire and the armistice that follows. Though Joe's mockery of her suggests that her failure to "connect" with him is due to her appropriation of a position that is not rightfully hers, his need to mock her and his feeling of relief after his success suggest her power over him. In the second movement, when Albert puts his hand on Joe, Joe follows the message of the hand on his shoulder. Subsequently, when Miss Stokes orders Albert to take his hands off Joe, Albert satirically replies, "Yes, Major." By jauntily agreeing to her "order," Albert mocks her attempt to appropriate a non-traditional assertive role just as he mocks her when he nicknames her "monkey-nuts"—though he never calls her so to her face. His fear of her, as well as his repeated failed attempts to be Joe's substitute, suggest that his nickname for her merely follows in the tradition of sexist name-calling. Like other instances of sexist name-calling in stories such as "The Witch a la Mode" and "The Primrose Path," this instance, too, perpetuates the patriarchal structure of social organization that allows such actions to persist. Albert's mockery thus allies him to Joe and gives both of them the strength to counter her power. But though the males in the unit succesfully silence Miss Stokes, their need to jeer and their need for each other to be able to jeer suggest their inability to cope with atypical female behavior.

In Miss Stokes Lawrence creates an image of a strong, assertive woman. Though the silence to which she is reduced by the men in the unit suggests their supremacy and perpetuates patriarchal attitudes toward women, the text is nevertheless undone by the men's need to bond with each other to silence her. Language accomplishes more than Lawrence may have understood; the immensity of the threat that women's independence poses for the patriarchy, riddled by fear and weakness, is revealed.

IV

"The Overtone," written in 1924, focuses on the unsatisfactory marriage relation of Mr. and Mrs. Renshaw and the lesson that Elsa Laskell, a young unmarried female, learns from their relation. In the beginning, Mrs. Renshaw, unable to be intimate with her husband, involves herself with the suffragette movement. At one of her scheduled meetings, Elsa Laskell feels as though she can hear more than the words themselves; she feels she can hear the "woman's heart" behind the words (747). Mrs. Renshaw, we are told, talks not because she has anything to say about subjects such as the State Endowment for mothers, but because she is burdened by despair and needs to relieve herself. Her words are like "inarticulate music" to the "heart" (748) of Elsa, who internalizes them. Like an observer, Elsa quietly sits and listens to the talk of Mrs. Renshaw and Mrs. Hankin; hers is "a silence of being" (748). But soon, because by hearing that which was not uttered she has been able to connect with her hostess, she is overwhelmed by her hostess's despair. Going out to the garden, she begins to cry because she is concerned for herself. At this point, Lawrence changes the direction of his narration by using Mr. Renshaw, who is in the garden, as a means to expound his ideas on Pan and Christ. At first, Mr. Renshaw himself feels despair at the death of Pan—in him. Though he tries to console Elsa by telling her that since Pan is dead, she need have no worry, he does not succeed. Because she identifies herself with the nymph, she does not want to die with Pan. She wants to be with a man. At this point, Mrs. Renshaw enters the garden and there follows a discussion on how Christ killed Pan. While Elsa reads in Pan's death Christ's fear of him, Mrs. Renshaw reads in it Pan's fear of Christ. From the discussion, Mr. Renshaw realizes that "Christ was woman, and Pan was man" (757). Elsa learns from the experience of Mr. and Mrs. Renshaw that the woman ascends to independence at the expense of the death of the man. She also learns that she does not want to weave the robe of death for the man in her life (as did Hercules's wife), but wants to flee only to be caught. Thus, because they both represent different types of love, she wants to embrace both Christ and Pan.

Just as Widmer dismisses "The Last Laugh" because of its use of "supernatural trickery," he also dismisses "The Overtone" as an example of a badly written story steeped in Biblical language and mythic references. Mrs. Renshaw conforms to Widmer's stereotype of the destructive woman who "has turned love into rape" (153). Further, Widmer interprets Mrs. Renshaw's concerns with women's rights as that of a "frigid wife" who uses "liberal idealism" to cover "personal inadequacy" (153). But we have come a long way since such interpretations of male-female sexual dissatisfaction were acceptable. Increasingly, people in general, and feminists in particular, are paying greater attention to reasons for sexual discontent within relationships. The frigid wife of earlier times now has a history within which she came into existence. For example, among others, Burness E. Moore, in "Psychoanalytic Meaning and

Treatment of Frigidity," suggests that often doubts about their own masculinity may cause some men to blame the woman for not being able to arouse them (68). Moore reminds us that "[i]n the Victorian period . . . the problem of frigidity itself was largely denied by a cultural attitude that saw enjoyment of sex as a male prerogative, not to be shared by a respectable woman. At present, the pendulum has swung in the opposite direction" (68). Today, many women insist that enjoyment of sex is a shared prerogative. But though many critics differ from Widmer and ascribe blame for lack of sexual response in women to the male, it is not my purpose here to apportion blame on either gender. It is more significant to my purpose that medical studies on lack of sexual responsiveness in women have created room for a further understanding of the Renshaws' marital relation, and of Elsa's understanding of, and response to, that relation.

In contrast to Widmer, Harris views Elsa in a line of female seekers in Lawrence's earlier fiction who reconcile within themselves male and female principles. For Lawrence the union of male and female principles does not exist within a single gender, but in the marriage between the two genders. Briefly, functioning as a sort of sequel to "The Last Laugh," "The Overtone" undoes the denouement of the last story. Unlike James in "The Last Laugh," Elsa, in "The Overtone," is willing to embrace the principles of both Pan and Christ, of both the flesh and of the spirit, of both taking and giving. By characterizing the female protagonist in his fiction as Isis in Search, Lawrence articulates his belief that human completion is achieved only in marriage. When his fictional men and women possess characteristics associated exclusively with either Pan or Christ, union is impossible. This story, then, serves as a thinly disguised forum for the presentation of ideas that Lawrence otherwise expresses covertly in his fiction or discusses pedantically in his non-fiction. By juxtaposing Mrs. Renshaw's sexual reticence, failed marital relation, and subsequent uninterested involvement with the suffraggettes with Elsa's decision to chase and be chased by a man, Lawrence portrays the women's cause as a weak and unhappy substitute for a woman's true desires and thus demonstrates the victory of the heterosexual relation.

But I believe that in the expressed need for the union of Pan and Christ, Lawrence demonstrably advocates androgyny. Though Lawrence demonstrates in his story Elsa's decision to embrace both Pan and Christ within a heterosexual relation, given the alternative life styles and choices that modern life offered, he also introduces here the possiblity of such a union within a single individual. Elsa, too, realizes that the union she must look for goes beyond that between opposite genders, for the man she embraces must be both Christ and Pan just as she must be both woman and nymph. Lawrence reiterates Elsa's realization by defining Christ and Pan as more than female and male principles; he also defines them as the principles of give and take. Since these latter behaviors are not determined by gender, they, then, may be assimilated within a single human being. This idea is especially significant in view of Lawrence's later treatment of the same theme in his short novel, *The Escaped Cock*.[59] Thus, Lawrence is extremely experimental in this story. Though he appears to align himself with the patriarchy by espousing the heterosexual, he also challenges patriarchy by espousing his belief in the union of what Pan and Christ represent.

***

My study of the unmarried female characters in the short stories illustrates that, here, Lawrence incorporates the impact of class on gender politics. In the last chapter I discussed Lawrence's portrayal of the virgin female characters from the middle-class. Since Lawrence believed that the hope of England's regeneration resided with the infusion of lower class vitality into the aristocracy, the younger unmarried female characters, in contrast to the older unmarried female characters, are presented as working-class women who are sexually liberated. Lawrence does not couch their sexual encounters in romantic terms, but, rather, often presents such encounters as a means of livelihood.

Not only does Lawrence distinguish between the older and younger unmarried female characters on the basis of their sexuality, but he also distinguishes between them on the basis of their speech. In contrast to his portrayal of the older unmarried women as silent, chattering, or mad, he depicts the younger unmarried women as more effectively outspoken. This outspokenness, however, ultimately serves them no useful purpose, for the younger unmarried female characters are also bested by the male characters, either by the protagonist or by a narrator who exposes an ironic conflict between their thought and action. Thus, their actions are often portrayed as borne out of vindictiveness, and contradictory to their presumed desires as androcentrically envisioned.

Further, though the younger unmarried female characters are sexually liberated and more assertive in their behavior, they do not define themselves in relation to other women. Rather, like their less assertive sisters, they continue to define themselves in relation to men. For example, Annie and the tram conductors define themselves in relation to John Thomas in "Tickets, Please," Miss Stokes defines herself in relation to Joe in "Monkey Nuts," and Elaine and the other young woman define themselves in relation to Sutton and the men they leave him for in "The Primrose Path." By defining themselves in relation to a male other, the young female characters in these stories are portrayed by Lawrence as similar to their older counterparts. Moreover, these later stories break away from the Christian symbolism that earlier defined characters as too giving or sacrificing, but to no avail. Their self-interest, no matter how sexually liberating, brings them no closer to happiness and satisfaction than does the self-denial and self-sacrifice of their older counterparts.

It is as if Lawrence motivates his younger unmarried female characters to stray outside of patriarchal bounds in order to show the dire consequences of such assertiveness. Lawrence seems much more exploratory in his construction of younger, as opposed to older, unmarried female characters, but there is less here than meets the eye. The younger characters' challenges to the patriarchy are not entirely successful, sometimes because of the women's own lack of strength of purpose. Yet that failure is often the result of patriarchal retaliation, designed to counter the threat posed by assertive women. Thus, the text reveals what is perhaps concealed from the essentialist Lawrence: the weakness, the gap, in the patriarchal structure that women will breach unless contained by force.

Chapter 4

The Short Novels

Following my focus on Lawrence's portrayal of unmarried female characters in the short stories, in this chapter I shall focus on the unmarried female characters in his short novels. Though critics have been rather silent regarding Lawrence's short stories in general and his portrayal of the unmarried female characters in the short stories in particular, they have been more voluble about them in relation to his short novels. For example, critics such as Kate Millett and Harry T. Moore have read the short novels in terms of a dynamics of control and a dialectic of male domination versus female submission. Further, many critics, from Middleton Murry (1931) to John Worthen (1991), have approached the impact of Lawrence's life on his short novels and analyzed the interconnection of themes within the novellas and more generally within all of Lawrence's fiction.[60] Since critics have bypassed, or treated marginally, the unmarried female characters in Lawrence's short novels, in this chapter I shall focus on characters such as Ellen March and Jill Banford in *The Fox*, Flora Manby in *St. Mawr*, Yvette Saywell and Aunt Cissie in *The Virgin and the Gipsy*, and Madeleine, the young female slave, the woman of Isis, and the man who died in *The Escaped Cock*.[61]

In this chapter, I demonstrate that just as in the short stories Lawrence evokes images of women from culture and myth to create parallels and contrasts with his fictional presentation of the unmarried females, so does he evoke similar images in the short novels. Further, just as both the older and younger female characters in the short stories are silenced by the patriarchy, so are they silenced and reduced to inaction by the patriarchy in the short novels. But Lawrence does not merely perpetuate images of patriarchy; he often experiments with presenting unmarried females in relations that challenge the patriarchy, but then brings such characters to defeat, as if explorations in non-patriarchal territory are undertaken to prove once again that patriarchy and essentialist understandings of the sexes are absolutes and Truth. For instance, with Ellen March and Jill Banford in *The Fox*, Lawrence experiments with lesbian relations. But though he presents these two older female characters from the rural middle-class as sexually liberated, he presents them in circumstances of defeat. His text validates the heterosexual union between March and Grenfel over the lesbian relation between March and Banford, and thus posits homosexuality not as a real option for women but as merely a deviant form of sexuality. With Flora Manby, a young female character from the upper-class in *St. Mawr*, Lawrence appears to celebrate the sexual liberation of the nineteen-twenties that allows her to have a public affair with a married man. Her sexual liberation, however, is diminished by being presented as callous and hurtful to others. Both Yvette and Aunt Cissie in *The Virgin and the Gipsy* represent middle-class rural life and function as counterparts to each other. With them, Lawrence echoes the medieval form of allegory that stereotypically associates youth and beauty with desire. Thus, in the tale, while the young and attractive Yvette represents desirable traits, the older Aunt Cissie represents less desirable traits. Further, in this tale, Lawrence appears to experiment in his presentation of women by evoking the image of the matriarchal system. Yet by presenting this system as debilitating not merely to the male but also to the female, he undermines the significance of such a system of social organization. Thus, in this tale, not only does Lawrence model his females as mere stereotypes, but his portrayal of females as independent of the patriarchy is so exaggerated and grotesque as to approach satire. Finally, in *The Escaped Cock*, Lawrence presents three images of unmarried females: Madeleine, the prostitute turned Saint, the young female slave, and the woman of Isis. In this tale, by resorting to his own private myth—as briefly explained in his short story "The Overtone"—Lawrence also evokes the image of the man who died, Christ, as both a male and a female character. But as in that story, such a presentation of female characters is problematic because it portrays them, finally, not as satisfied in themselves but as seekers after heterosexual relations. It defines the female, again, in relation to the male, denying her an independent existence. Consequently, the man who died and has now risen overlooks the significance of the transformation of Madeleine from whore to Madonna. He even overlooks his own transformation from being the representative of the female principle as Christ-crucified to being the representative of the male principle as the resurrected Christ to validate his own union with the woman of Isis. With the woman of Isis, Lawrence apppears to have come to an end of his phase of experimentation. With her, he evokes Greco-Christian myth to portray an essentialist image of Woman in search of her mate, or Isis in Search.

Lawrence is much more experimental in his presentation of the sexuality of unmarried female characters in the short novels than he was in the short stories. No longer does he frame them within the stereotypes of madonnas or whores, but combines these images in a single unmarried woman—Madeleine. Further, portraying unmarried women within a lesbian relation, or under a matriarchal system of social organization, allows him to question the idea of what it is to be a "woman." Such experimentation thus allows him to question his own essentialist claims about women, and demonstrates his constant struggle with the patriarchy. His historical period thus forces him to pose questions about essentialist positions, but he always returns to his starting point.

I

The Fox, begun in 1918, was finally finished in 1921. In the interim between start and finish, following his usual writing practice, Lawrence lengthened and changed the end.[62] This tale focuses on a triangular relationship among Ellen March, Jill Banford, and Henry Grenfel. March and Banford are both almost thirty. Lawrence tells us that "[t]hey [are] neither of them young: that is, they [are] near thirty" (135). He also tells us that because Banford is plain looking and delicate in health, she has no prospects of marriage. Knowing this, her father gives her a start in life by providing her with a house. March goes to live with Banford. Being "more robust" and having "learned carpentry and joinery," March will "be the man about the place" (135). While, initially, they have Banford's old grandfather living with them, after his death they are on their own.

Into this female arena comes a young man, Henry Grenfel, who is about twenty years old. He is the grandson of the man from whom Banford's father had bought the farm. In the beginning, it is Banford who encourages him to stop for the night with them, but he soon ends up staying, and working, for them. She sees him as a means of protecting them from the isolation of their surroundings and as manpower to hunt the fox that has been hunting their hens. But when Banford notices Grenfel's attraction to March, she becomes very jealous and wants him to leave. She even advises March against him. Grenfel, however, overhears the conversation and determines to "get" March. Just as he successfully hunts and skins the fox, he hunts and captures March. Though he is unable to persuade March to marry him before he leaves, he is able to convince her to become engaged. Because soon after his return to camp March writes and breaks off their engagement, Grenfel is deeply distressed and rushes back to confront her. On his return, he finds March trying to cut down an old tree while Banford and her parents watch the proceedings. He takes over. He knows that if he cuts in a certain way, the tree will fall on Banford. Since he wants this to happen, he follows his thoughts. But though he cuts the tree, he covers his devious action by shouting to caution Banford. When Banford ignores him, she is hit by the tree and dies.

Though critics such as Widmer and Harris continue to read *The Fox* as a parallel to "You Touched Me" (1919) in its thematic concerns and in its plot structure, Harris also departs from Widmer to discuss Ian Gregor's work on this tale as one of the earliest contributions in challenging the work's denouement as the victory of life over death. In the line of Gregor and Harris, I, too, consider the ending "unprepared for and unjustified" (Harris 163) and question the nature of male victory at the end of this tale. But I also believe that regardless of the problematic nature of the ending, of significance is that *both* March and Banford are weakened, silenced, and finally defeated by Grenfel. March, especially, is portrayed by Lawrence to be dependent on Grenfel. For example, from the start, March in the presence of Grenfel, like Matilda in the presence of Hadrian in "You Touched Me," stands paralyzed. "She did not know why *she could not move*. . . . It was as in a dream when the heart strains and the body cannot stir," says the narrator (*The Fox* my italics 184). Further, March's characteristic response in Grenfel's vicinity is one of weakness. Lawrence tells us that "[t]he moment she saw his glowing red face it was all over with her. She was as *helpless* as if she had been *bound*" (my italics 196). She also has a desire to be saved. "She want[s] the boy to *save* her" (my italics 189). The italicized words suggest March's helplessness and relinquishment of agency and choice to the male. Here, not only does Lawrence portray March as unable to act of her own volition, but he also portrays her as *willing* her own lack of volition. Further, not only does March wish to be saved, but she wishes to be saved by a "boy." By using the term "boy" for Grenfel, Lawrence appears to emphasize March's dependence on him. Lawrence evokes this response by encouraging a comparison of the term "boy" for Grenfel with his previous use of the term "girl"—with its derogatory associations in culture—for female characters such as Miss Wrexall in "Two Blue Birds." But studies such as Julia Penelope's on the origins of language inform us that no particular derogatory associations surround the use of this term for a male character as compared to the use of the term "girl" for a female character. Penelope explains that though the term "boi" "appeared in writing in Middle English (ME) around 1300, . . . its original sense remains uncertain" (98). She is only able to trace its roots "to a similar term in E. Frisian that meant 'young gentleman'" (98). But though inferences drawn from Penelope's study suggest there are no stereotypical negative cultural associations between Lawrence's use of the term "boy" and Grenfel, I believe that the term "boy" does remind us of the ten-year age difference between him and March and emphasizes her weakness and dependence in relation to him despite being older than him. Lawrence reinforces the idea of March's dependence on Grenfel through the metaphor of the fox and hen or the hunter and his quarry in relation to them. Since, from the beginning, March has associated Grenfel with the fox and herself with his quarry, the text now suggests that the maximum hope for the quarry to protect herself from the hunter lies in her leaving herself at his mercy.

Though Lawrence tries to present March's dependence on Grenfel in a positive light, he fails. For instance, the tale suggests that after Banford is felled like an old tree, her sterility will be replaced by something more fruitful—the relation between Grenfel and March. I believe that Lawrence emphasizes this possibility in the metaphoric significance of the three names. Banford's name can be associated with the idea of banishment, Grenfel's name can be associated with the cutting of the "green" or tree, and March's name can be associated with spring time. In the tale, after Banford's death, Grenfel is able to marry March and take her away with him to his camp. By exhibiting Grenfel's demand for complete submission from March at the end, Lawrence creates a parallel between this tale and *The Captain's Doll* where Captain Hepburn demands complete submission from Hannele. But the final scene of *The Fox* is as problematic as that of *The Captain's Doll.* The narrator tells us that though Grenfel has "won" March, he has not "got" her (200). The narrator also tells us that Grenfel "want[s] to veil her [March's] woman's spirit, as Orientals veil the woman's face" (204). Grenfel's desire to veil March's spirit—a spirit that he specifically associates with women and independence—suggests that the struggle between March and Grenfel implicates more than just them; it implicates all men and women. Further, by evoking the Oriental's use of the veil in culture, Lawrence introduces the idea of Grenfel's patriarchal desire to remove March from the gaze of the "other" males. In feminist terms, the image of the veil as used by Grenfel translates itself into an image of the patriarchal imposition of silence on women, given the role of the veil in many cultures. As Anny Tual explains in "Speech and Silence: Women in Iran," just as the veil conceals the female face—and by extension, the entire body—from the male gaze, so does silence prevent the female voice from troubling the male (*Visibility and Power* 54-69).[63]

Because the female characters in both *The Fox* and *The Captain's Doll* are conflicted by their feelings of desire and reluctance to cede authority to the males, their decision to submit at the end appears to be externally imposed by Lawrence. The forged nature of the two endings suggests the possible failure of the male protagonists's desire to silence the female. But because, after all, both the tales do end with the submission—however reluctant—of the females to the males and because Lawrence does present the female characters' passivity and silence as a distinct possibility, we must take such a portrayal of female characters into account. For example, at the end, though March feels enervated by Grenfel's persistence to make her submit to him, she also feels the desire to express her attraction to him in some way. But she is aware that Grenfel does not want such an overt expression of love from her. He wants her "to be passive, to acquiesce, and to be submerged under the surface of love" (*The Fox* 201). At this point, she likens her life to that of a seaweed, never rising above the surface of the water until death brings her above the surface as a lifeless corpse. She knows that "she, being a woman, must be like that" (202). Among other things, the image of being submerged and leading an under-water life evokes a theme of suffocation, silence, and strangulation. And the only escape she sees from such an existence is a release in death that suggests another kind of submergence—only more permanent.

Lawrence also portrays the conflict in March through the metaphor of clothes. In the beginning, March appropriates a typical male role and garb in her relationship with Banford.[64] Soon, Lawrence tells us that just like Matilda's desire for Hadrian in "You Touched Me," March's desire for Grenfel in *The Fox* is expressed in her dreams. Once she acknowledges her attraction to Grenfel in her dream, however, she changes her trousers for a dress and stockings. To many critics, March's change of clothes suggests her recognition and appropriation of her true role as woman. R. P. Draper, for example, sees the change as signifying that "she is not really a masculine type" (125). Draper also implies that because March's choice to wear trousers is as unnatural as her and Banford's desire to live independently on the farm, she and Banford are unable to kill the intrusive other—either the fox or Grenfel. While Draper's suggestion places March and Banford in the line of "cocksure women," I believe that Lawrence's presentation of these characters is far more subtle. By depicting Grenfel as ultimately victorious and by presenting his victory as subconsciously desired by the female despite associating Grenfel with an animal, Lawrence mitigates the negative association with Grenfel and thus muddies interpretation.

Unlike March, Banford is not conflicted about her feelings (for March or Grenfel) and is willing to assume responsibility for her choice. Banford tries, as in any heterosexual relationship, to retain the established status quo between herself and March when she feels it threatened by the intrusion of Grenfel, much as the fox threatens the peace of the farm. It is significant, however, that it is March and not Banford who makes the connection between Grenfel and the fox:

> He was identified with the fox—and he was here in full presence. She need not go after him any more. There in the shadow of her corner she gave herself up to a warm, relaxed peace, almost like sleep, accepting the spell that was on her. But she wished to remain hidden. She was only fully at peace whilst he forgot her, talking to Banford. Hidden in the shadow of the corner, she need not any more be divided in herself, trying to keep up two planes of consciousness. She could at last lapse into the odour of the fox. (*The Fox* 147)

Lawrence informs us that Grenfel, who is "a huntsman in spirit, not a farmer, and not a soldier stuck in a regiment" (154), has decided on his "quarry" (154), March. Because Grenfel is interested in "getting" March, critics have primarily focused on the significance of their relation. But it is equally significant that, especially after actually killing the fox, Grenfel appears to assume the role of the predatory fox in his relations with the two females. By threatening the equanimity of both Banford and March's existence, he becomes the fox and they his victims. But though Lawrence portrays both Banford and March as victims of Grenfel, he distinguishes between them by adopting different metaphors to describe them. While he associates March with the deer (153) and the hare (154), he associates Banford with birds, like the geese (199). While March—like the deer and the hare—is mesmerized by Grenfel's gaze (153-54, 196), Banford—like a bird—avoids meeting Grenfel's eye (158).

While the metaphoric associations of March with the hare and deer have occasioned readings that either identify her as Grenfel's victim or align her with him,[65] critics continue to ignore the significance of Banford as the unidentified quarry of Grenfel. Just as Grenfel silences March, so does he silence Banford. Indeed, his silencing of Banford is far more complete, for it is the silence of death to which he reduces her. Not only does Grenfel hunt her down finally, much as a fox kills a hen, but he murders her in the full awareness that his happiness with March depends on his ability to eliminate the threat of Banford's presence. "In his heart he had decided her death," writes Lawrence (198). By portraying Grenfel's recognition of the threat of March's relation with Banford as a threat to his relation with March, Lawrence portrays the threat that (female) homosexuality represents to the patriarchy. He also suggests that hens, like March, rightfully belong with cocks, like Grenfel.

In brief, Banford's disposition and physical limitations circumscribe her within a conventional female position of looking after the hearth and home, just as they define March's physically more dominant role (135). To George J. Becker, this difference in disposition between the two women characters suggests their lesbian relation (125). If we accept readings of critics such as Becker and view the relation between the two females as a lesbian one in this text, then, Lawrence appears to present unmarried women in a role different from that of the stereotypical "Lady of Shallott"—the figure of the woman as sexually reticent. He also *appears* to offer women a choice beyond the conventional heterosexual relation. While some critics welcome Lawrence's portrayal of lesbianism as an experiment with female sexuality, most critics are suspicious of or dissatisfied with his portrayal of female homosexuality, especially in relation to the portrayal of male homosexuality in his other fiction. For example, Barbara Hardy, in "Women in D. H. Lawrence's Works," compares Lawrence's portrayals of male and female homosexuality to conclude that Lawrence "yearns after touch and tenderness in male friendships but finds Lesbianism repulsive" (90). Widmer also finds Lawrence's portrayal of female homosexuality dissatisfying. He believes that "in Lawrence's fictions [female] homosexual relations defeat hope and love, perhaps because of a narcissism that lacks the creativeness of genuine polarity" (59). E. W. Tedlock seconds Widmer's interpretation and views the fox, who is associated with Grenfel, as "the totem of the lower class man who breaks up this unholy alliance" (116-17).

In contrast to critics like Hardy, Widmer, and Tedlock, Harris defends Lawrence's presentation of female-female relationships. She asserts that Lawrence has been wrongly accused of shying away from presenting such relationships. According to her, it is a mark of Lawrence's genius that he is able to present in his *oeuvre* female-female relationships that may be either natural and healthful or claustrophobic and unnatural. Harris asserts that the March-Banford relation in *The Fox* and the Matilda-Emmie relation in "You Touched Me" are two examples of unnatural and claustrophobic female relationships (166-70). But I believe that the examples Harris posits as favorable presentations of female friendship such as Ursula and Gudrun in *Women in Love*, Connie Chatterley and Ivy Bolton in *Lady Chatterley's Lover*, Lou and her mother, Mrs. Witt, in *St. Mawr* are not examples of lesbian relationships. Because critics such as Harris fail to distinguish between a female friendship and a lesbian relationship, it is necessary to re-assess Lawrence's treatment of Banford within the context of a lesbian relation.[66]

Lawrence often articulated his thoughts on same-sex relations. For instance, in a letter to Katherine Mansfield, in 1918, Lawrence had written that he believed in an eternal friendship, like a marriage bond, between "man and man" as well as between "women and women," but that he had "not met or formed any such friendship" (*Collected Letters* I 565). In this letter, Lawrence seems to accept a desire within himself to form such relationships; but as opposed to critics like Widmer and Tedlock who equate Lawrence's homosexual longings with his sexual identity, and assume that his sexual preference is the basis for his "biased" presentation of female-female relations, I do not believe Lawrence's acknowledgement of homosexual desire proves, conclusively, the existence of any such relation in his own life at this time.[67] In concurrence with John Worthen, I believe that Lawrence's more comfortable attitude toward male friendships can be understood in terms of his inhibited upbringing at home. Worthen explains that not only did such friendships arouse no violent reactions at home, but they were also Lawrence's means of sublimating unsettling feelings about sex, which appeared to him to be dangerously similar to violence. Thus, Worthen distinguishes between Lawrence the man who may experience and even express homosexual longings, and Lawrence the man who may actually participate in such a relation. Worthen correctly says that there is no necessary correlation between the two (156-58).

But despite studies such as Worthen's, many critics fail to appreciate the experimental nature of Lawrence's portrayal of female homosexuality. This reluctance in critics to evaluate Lawrence's contribution reflects society's attitude toward homosexual relations, particularly between women. Clearly, although recent studies trace the homosexual novel to the nineteenth century, it is only over the last few decades that homosexuality has begun to be treated more openly in literature and culture. This reticence about homosexual longings is even more exaggerated in the realm of female homosexuality. For example, tracing the treatment of women in history who refused to define themselves in relation to men, Adrienne Rich says they "were tortured and burned as witches, slandered in religious and later in 'scientific' tracts, portrayed in art and literature as bizarre, amoral, destructive, decadent women" (225).[68] As a result of the threat that homosexuality—both female and male—represents to most people who have been conditioned to the ideology of patriarchy, in the past it was often presented in fiction within an alien setting. For instance, James D. Riemer, in "Homosexuality in Science Fiction and Fantasy," explains how "[h]omosexuality may seem less threatening to the average reader if it is presented as an aspect of a distant future or an alien culture rather than as an issue confronting the reader in his or her own society" (145).[69]

Still, though biological and psychological studies in this area have contributed in furthering today's public awareness and tolerance of homosexuality, the fear and threat that it represents for the patriarchy has not entirely been overcome. The threat that female homosexuality evokes in the patriarchy is especially evident in the current patriarchal conflation of the terms "spinster" and "lesbian." Feminists challenge this conflation to offer their own definitions. For instance, Adrienne Rich, opposing patriarchal definitions of these terms, asserts that a lesbian is one who chiefly bonds closely with women and against men. But Catherine Stimpson differs from Rich and asserts that a lesbian is one who finds another woman sexually attractive (in Doan 5). While Laura Doan does not offer her own definition of a "lesbian," she uses both Rich's and Stimpson's definitions to show the fallacy in patriarchal conflation—because in contrast, a spinster defines herself in relation to no other (4-5). But despite these different understandings, both terms are loaded with derogatory associations in patriarchal structures of social organization because in each case the woman defines herself and asserts her right to remain separate from the male.

The desire to define herself as separate from the male is less apparent in March than in Banford. In the beginning, Lawrence tells us that March dresses like a male and speaks in low tones. Her clothes and her manner suggest that she has assumed the role of the male in her relation with Banford. But the March-Banford relationship as represented by March is made ambiguous by the fact that we never enter their consciousness on a frank discussion of the subject of their relation. For instance, at the end, we know that March wishes to be saved but we do not know what she desires to be saved from. The action does not reveal whether it is Banford's presence or her own lesbian desires for Banford that oppress her. We know that the tale's denouement focuses on March's troubled thoughts regarding her past—her relationship with Banford, and her future—the terrible *agon* between her and Grenfel over her desire to assume the power of choice and responsibility (*The Fox* 204). We also know that March's struggle to retain her independent spirit despite Grenfel's efforts to "veil her spirit" (204) conflicts with her desire to give up the struggle against Grenfel, just as her earlier fear of Banford and her desire to be saved from her (189) conflicts with her later realization of her inability to make Banford really happy. But we do not know for sure, despite her conflict over Banford and Grenfel (March describes both struggles as attempts to achieve something just beyond her grasp [202]), whether, truly attracted to a life with Banford, she is nevertheless merely succumbing to the patriarchy by choosing Grenfel.

In contrast to March, Banford defines herself as separate from the male. But Lawrence presents this difference in stereotypical terms. In brief, unlike March, who is mesmerized by Grenfel's glance, Banford does not like to look at him (158). Her clothes and language further define her difference. Banford is more feminine in her attire and is more talkative. While "March seems to listen, in her distant, manly way," "Banford *chat[s]* easily" (my italics 139). While March is "robust" in her speech (178), Banford murmurs (177) and is "plaintive" (178). Lawrence also suggests a metaphoric association between Banford and a bird. "Banford . . . love[s] nothing so much as *gossip*, and . . . [is] full of perky interest, like a *bird*," writes Lawrence (my italics 145). When Grenfel tells Banford that March has agreed to marry him, she looks at March "like a bird that has been shot: *a poor little sick bird*" (my italics 165). At the end, as Grenfel plans Banford's death, he looks "into the sky, like a huntsman who is watching a flying *bird*" (my italics 198). Later, he looks at her dead body "as he would watch *a wild goose* he had shot. Was it winged, or dead?" (my italics 199). The words in italics evoke stereotypical presentations of women in culture. Cheris Kramarae's observation again obtains: the patriarchy often labels women speakers as "*shrews, bitches, cats, hens; shrill, sharp-tongued, and gossipy*" (xiii). Grenfel's attitude toward Banford and Lawrence's descriptive language, associating Banford with a bird and her speech with chatter and gossip, draw on derogatory patriarchal terms to label women speakers, trivialize their speech, and minimize their significance and strength.

Lawrence also emphasizes Banford's desire for March and her helplessness in Grenfel's presence in other ways. For example, during the course of the tale, Banford's actions and attitudes toward March and Grenfel appear to be motivated by her desire to hold on to March. But the tale suggests Banford's inability to succeed in keeping March away from Grenfel. Like Emmie, in "You Touched Me," Banford expresses her inadequacy in keeping March away from Grenfel when she bursts into tears. Further, Lawrence tells us that when Grenfel speaks with "anger," "contempt," and "fury" to Banford as compared to the "tenderness" and "proud authority" with which he speaks to March—to which the latter responds—Banford's "thin shoulders sh[ake] in an agony of weeping" (*The Fox* 183). Though Banford's tears suggest her strong feeling for March, they also suggest her defeat by Grenfel by showing her as incapable of action against him. Further, they suggest that in many ways her murder is only the final nail that Grenfel drives into the coffin, for by creating a doubt in March's mind about the correctness of her feelings for Banford he has already begun to "kill" her.

In this tale, even as Lawrence appears to challenge patriarchy by depicting Banford and March in a lesbian relation, Lawrence perpetuates patriarchal stereotypes by presenting Banford as weak and ineffective. Though Lawrence's portrayal of lesbianism shows his willingness to explore and probe past patriarchal descriptions of unmarried women and demonstrates his continuing struggle with the patriarchy and the mysteries of sexuality, the story does not finally validate homosexuality. The story in fact diminishes the value of homosexuality by portraying lesbian desire in March as ambiguous and a desire to be superceded by Grenfel's more predatory—and successful—heterosexual challenge. In a final turn of the screw, however, the association of Grenfel's success with predatoriness unmasks the pervasive power of patriarchy and its insidiousness.

II

St. Mawr, written in 1924, is a tale that focuses on the relationship between Lou and Rico, who soon after their marriage become bored with each other. As a consequence of the weakness of their relation, Lou turns to horse riding and draws closer to her mother, Mrs. Witt, and Rico turns to other women, especially Flora.[70] One day, when Lou sees a stallion, St. Mawr, and is fascinated by it, she decides to overlook the violent history of the animal and purchase him for her husband. But the horse, living up to his violent history, resists Rico's efforts to control him and finally throws him. A furious Rico plans to sell the horse to his lover, Flora. When Lou hears that Flora plans to geld St. Mawr, she is outraged and decides to send the horse away with her mother.

At this time, both mother and daughter have disillusioning experiences with their horse-groomsmen. Lewis, St. Mawr's groom, refuses to marry Mrs. Witt, and Lou refuses to have a relationship with Phoenix, Mrs. Witt's horse's groom. Both females now decide to buy a ranch in America. Rico responds with outrage at Lou's decision to move to America, even though he himself has been recovering from his fall from St. Mawr at Flora's house. But at the end, disregarding Rico's anger, Lou leaves with her mother for America. Lawrence ends the tale by focusing on Lou and Mrs. Witt's experiences in America and their realization about male-female relations.

Though both *St. Mawr* and *The Ladybird* have elicited much critical interest as prime examples of narrative from Lawrence's leadership phase—a phase in which Lawrence focused on the leader-follower theme in gender relations, *St. Mawr* focuses briefly on two unmarried female characters—Flora Manby and Laura.[71] The chief unmarried female character in this tale is Flora Manby. Since the text does not offer us any definite information about her relation with Rico, Lou's husband, we can only guess about her reasons for having a relation with him. Though Lou deals with this humiliation by ignoring it in public, she often vents her feelings in private to her mother in letters (379-84). My focus, however, is not on how Lou deals with her husband's extra-marital affair, but on Lawrence's presentation of Flora's attitude toward participating—publicly—in an affair with a married man. Since she is aware of the strained relations between Rico and Lou, we could speculate that, perhaps, she hopes for his divorce and their own subsequent marriage. In any case, from the start Flora is aware of the changing times and her unmarried state in these times. She feels exhilarated about living in a time that allows women to express themselves sexually. In this regard she tells Rico, "I think this is the best age there ever was for a girl to have *a good time* in" (my italics 336). She also thanks her stars that she "live[s] in nineteen-twenty odd, not in some other beastly date when a woman had to cringe before mouldy domineering men" (336). Her sexual liberation is no doubt her gesture of rebellion before the patriarchy that she identifies as "mouldy domineering men." That her relationship with Rico is publicly recognized and that each visits the other's home openly express both her sexual freedom and her personal freedom.

The text suggests that Flora Manby is a decisive young woman who knows what she wants. Though David Holbrook asserts that by associating Flora with St. Mawr's emasculation, Lawrence satirizes English middle-class hatred of life in all its "power, danger, and beauty" (115), I believe that in this tale Lawrence evokes more than a sense of class hatred. I believe that her decision to have a relation with Rico may be seen in parallel with her decision to geld the stallion, St. Mawr, once she has him in her possession. By using this metaphor, Lawrence evokes a parallel between Flora and cocksure women and another between Rico and hensure men. Just as the female characters in "The Primrose Path" and

"Tickets, Please," Flora, too, is presented as appropriating a traditionally male position. That Lawrence finds her behavior unacceptable is apparent from the fact that the tale suggests that just like a "cocksure woman,"[72] Flora's strength leads to Rico's weakness; just as she intends to emasculate the horse, she emasculates Rico. Lawrence especially suggests her devouring nature by naming her "Manby," which carries connotations of predatoriness and her desire/effort "to be a man". But just as in the previous stories (such as "Monkey Nuts") when Lawrence portrayed female characters as appropriating male positions, so in this tale such a portrayal merely proves that what is reprehensible in male behavior is equally reprehensible in female behavior. Therefore, though Flora's behavior may be perceived as liberated in this tale, it is still reprehensible because though Flora successfully expresses her sexual liberation, her actions are portrayed as thoughtless, vicious, and hurtful to Lou.

Angered by Flora's behavior, Lou wonders what the Manby girls[73] actually want: "Undermine, undermine, undermine. They want . . . to undermine Rico." She thinks that they "[b]elieve in nothing, care about nothing: but keep the surface easy, and have a good time" (341). She associates their behavior with the "mysterious potency of evil" (341). Lou sees barrenness and cruelty as a dominant trait in the characters of both (361). She also associates Flora with fox-hunting (362) and Rico with Priapus (381).[74] Though Lou's observations are not unbiased, they suggest her awareness of Rico and Flora's behavior and serve as commentary on both their actions. In addition to David Holbrook, who interprets Lou's denunciation as an evidence of Lawrence's misogyny (117), I believe that Lou's denunciation of the Manby females suggests Lawrence's often conflicting and unresolved attitude toward unmarried women. This lack of resolution is especially apparent in Lawrence's use of the metaphor of the fox.

So far, in both *The Fox* and *St. Mawr*, Lawrence adopts the metaphor of the fox for the hunter as well as the hunted. Just as in *The Fox* Lawrence portrays March as both Grenfel's quarry and his partner in crime, so in *St. Mawr* does Lawrence portray Rico as both the hunter and the quarry of Flora Manby. For instance, when Lawrence refers to Flora as the "fox-hunting one" (*St. Mawr* 362), he seems to associate both Flora and Rico with the fox. Not only is Flora like a fox on the hunt with Rico as her victim in her castrating clutches, but she is also hunting for the fox, who is, we are told by Mrs. Witt, already castrated. Seeing her daughter unhappy because of Rico's unfaithfulness and disregard for her feelings, Mrs. Witt considers his behavior weak and unmanly and therefore like that of a castrated fox. Consequently, she tells Lou to inform Flora that she "may have [her] husband" for he "won't need emasculating" (361). Significantly, both March in *The Fox* and Flora in this tale are associated with a fox only when they've assumed the role of male predator. But since Lawrence associates both male and female characters in his fiction with the fox, we may assume that he implicates both men and women equally in predatory action. Again, female characters as imitators of masculine traits that are undesirable does not affirm the woman's cause but rather, suggests that hens in cock's clothing are part of a destructive masquerade.

In contrast to Flora, Lou's unmarried friend, Laura, looks young and virginal despite being in her late twenties. Lawrence tells us that when she talks to Lewis, the groom, she has "a slight, impertinent elvish smile on her virgin face" (392). Lawrence also emphasizes her virginity by evoking the story of the Laurel myth in relation to her name. Not only is she presented as sexually innocent, but Lawrence exaggerates her innocence when he presents the exhuberance with which she asks Lewis if he is really not afraid of St. Mawr. "Aren't you, *really*!—And can you always master him?" she asks the groom (392). Yet her fascination with St. Mawr and her father's hunters, which, because of her gender, she has never been allowed to ride by her father (393), suggest her latent maturity and sexuality. As a mature woman she correctly finds her father's discrimination "disgraceful" (393). Lawrence thus presents her as a combination of child and woman. Though Lawrence's Freudian association of sexuality with a fascination with horses is well-known,[75] because no further details surround the character of Laura, I shall limit myself to observing that Lawrence sets up the older female's inhibited and unexpressed sexuality as a brief contrast to that of the young and sexually liberated Flora. Moreover, since a symbolic reading of the episode with the horses suggests that her father is the cause of her inhibited sexuality, we may infer that he, in effect, has silenced the expression of her sexual self. Further, if we read the mouth, again, figuratively, as the mouth of the vagina, then Laura's father has silenced not only the expression of his daughter's sexuality, but also her speech.

In this tale, though Lawrence portrays a conventional brief sketch of a silenced Laura, he draws upon the experimental women of his time, unmarried females like his Flora Manby, the sexually liberated female of the nineteen-twenties. He shows Flora participating in the sexual revolution. But by portraying her as a maneater (as "Manby"), and women's liberation as predatory,[76] he also shows that while such a revolution may be personally liberating, socially it is as hurtful and reprehensible as any such act performed by the patriarchy. In other words, just as Rico's sexual liberation is gained at the expense of his wife, so is Flora's sexual liberation gained at the expense of Lou. Lawrence thus demonstrates that when women appropriate stereotypically male behaviors, they also deserve to be measured by the same yardstick.

III

The Virgin and the Gipsy, written in 1926 and published posthumously, is a tale that focuses on two characters, Yvette and the gipsy, who represent disparate backgrounds. The struggle between these characters functions as the basis for a confrontation between two opposing ways of life. The drama begins when the wife of the Vicar, Mr. Saywell, runs away with an impoverished young man. "She-who-was-Cynthia" leaves behind her two young daughters, Yvette and Lucille, a husband, and a legacy of bitterness. Soon after her departure, the Vicar's old widowed mother and unmarried brother and sister step in to make up for any lapses in the children's moral education. They interpret the mother's "selfishness and degraded lust" (473) as a betrayal of acceptable family and social mores, and hold it up as a blight of improper behavior from which the children need to be protected.

With this judgement in mind, the older relatives provide the children with an education that, though intensive, leaves them "quite the usual thing, tall young creatures with fresh, sensitive faces and bobbed hair and young-manly, deuce-take-it manners" (476). On returning from finishing school, Yvette is bored by the quiet life that she and her sister are expected to lead, especially with the type of men who surround them—men who fawn over and adore them. She wants a man she can fall in love with violently, and she wants to marry. Further, at this time Yvette defines her difference from the "old maids" by rebelling against her Aunt Cissie and any activities organized by such women as her aunt (478). Consequently, she would prefer being with the working men, but since "they [are] in another world" (478), she likes to visit their wives instead. Lucille, on the other hand, likes being adored and is sure that she would not like to fall violently in love. Lawrence suggests that she is more independent than Yvette, for she soon gets herself a job in the city as a private secretary, while Yvette continues to live her round of social occasions.

One day, on one of their usual motor jaunts with their friends, they encounter a young gipsy riding a cart while an old woman walks along the wayside with him. When the young men in the car rudely ask him to get out of their way, the gipsy instead calmly offers to read the women's fortune. Since the women respond eagerly to the gipsy's offer, everyone decides to take a break. Both Lucille and Yvette are told that they will marry in a few years. But in the tale the incident with the gipsy takes a backseat when Aunt Cissie discovers that Yvette has expropriated the church fund for her personal use. Though the affair blows over, Yvette feels hatred toward her family—especially toward her Aunt. Just like Yvette, Lucille, too, feels alienated within her surroundings when, one day, she is driven to rage against their grandmother in defense of their mother. She is further enraged with her aunt, who, though herself chafing against her own mother's dictatorship, is horrified by Lucille's behavior and orders her upstairs.

This humdrum pattern of existence continues for the two young women till, one day, Leo, Yvette's friend, proposes marriage to her. Overcome by indifference and bored by Leo's persistence, Yvette decides to take up the gipsy's earlier invitation to visit him at his camp. There, as they sit warming their hands by the fire, they see a car stop from which a young Jewess and her companion alight. The Jewess is Mrs. Fawcett, wife of a rich man who is divorcing her. Meanwhile, she's holidaying with Major Eastwood before they get married. Since this couple share an unconventional relationship, Yvette decides to keep her friendship with them secret. But she can not do so for very long. When her family finds out about her new friends, Mr. Saywell asks her to choose between them and her family. Yvette submits to family law till one Friday afternoon, while sitting alone in the garden, she suddenly hears someone shouting. It is the gipsy warning her of an approaching flood. As he runs forward to save her, they scramble together to safety after great difficulty. When the water enters the rectory, they seek shelter in Yvette's bedroom, where they finally consummate their passion. The next day Yvette wakes up alone to the sound of a policeman outside her window. Climbing through her window, he finds Yvette safe and discovers the grandmother's body floating in the water downstairs. The gipsy is nowhere to be seen. Lawrence informs us that the gipsy finally sends Yvette a farewell note informing her of his name, which she had not known till now.

While Yvette, the Vicar's younger daughter, is the key female protagonist of this tale, she is not the only unmarried female character in this story. Lucille, her older sister, and Aunt Cissie, who is over forty and is their father's unmarried sister, also contribute to the dramatic action. Though both Yvette and Lucille are very young at the time of the action (Yvette is nineteen and Lucille is twenty-one at the beginning of the action, which spans two years), I have included them in my study to contrast Lawrence's presentation of them with that of Aunt Cissie. Further, these young females represent through their experiences the conflict caused by changing social mores in the lives of the middle-class.

Most of the criticism surrounding this tale takes its lead from the title and focuses on the relation between Yvette and the gipsy and the significance of their final union. For example, Widmer describes *The Virgin and the Gipsy* as a parable of regeneration. This interpretation is especially clear in Lawrence's association of both Major Eastwood and the gipsy with the resurrected Christ. As the Major tells Yvette, both he and the gipsy nearly died during the war, but were somehow "resurrected" (*The Virgin and the Gipsy* 531). Later, Yvette, in her thoughts, equates her denial of the gipsy with Peter's denial of Christ before the third cock crew. In typical Lawrencean fashion, by obvious relation between the "cock" and the penis, the subsequent action also conflates two kinds of passion: the religious and the phallic (178-87).[77]

Not only does Widmer correctly note the conflation of the religious and secular elements in the Lawrencean oeuvre, but, in addition, John Humma views the gipsy as "the inheritor of the pagan ethic" (79). Humma believes that "[t]hough [Lawrence] establishes no direct link between the gipsy and Pan[,] . . . the Pan-nature is present and active in the person of Joe Boswell [the gipsy]" (79). This suggestion of an association suggests a conflation of Christian and pagan myth that is more obviously developed in *The Escaped Cock*. Further, such an association, also indicates Lawrence's fictional movement toward androgyny in the figure of the risen Lord—an idea that I shall, once again, discuss in relation to Lawrence's last novella.

Because the focus of past readings has been on the relationship between Yvette and the gipsy, the other female characters have been overlooked.[78] Further, I believe that the relation between Yvette and the gipsy is especially significant when we read it within the parameters of the patriarchal and matriarchal systems that are set up within the text. Since the patriarchal law, both secular and religious, centers in the figure of the rector, and even he is silenced under his mother's rule, it would be useful to focus briefly on the presentation of matriarchy in this tale.

E. W. Tedlock, in his discussion of the female characters in this tale, posits that it sets up a "matriarchy which is based on denial of vital human reality" (207). He shows how the gipsy, by contrast, is the master in his camp. But in order to understand Lawrence's portrayal of matriarchy, we first need to understand this concept in its historical context. Helen Diner offers us one approach to understanding matriarchy as a social system of organization. She explains that women's history, both in myth and culture, can be traced to a period of matriarchy. In *Mothers and Amazons*, Diner asserts that "[i]n the beginning there was woman" (1). She believes that

> [v]irgin conception reaches far into our animal ancestry as parthogenesis, through epochs incomparably longer than those that have passed since its termination. . . . [T]he original female in the animal species not only reproduces herself but also is the sole creatress of the male; the male is never anything without the female. Thread worms, wheel animalcules, plant lice, and many branchiopodia, as well as diverse types of wasps and butterflies are all virginal mothers. Parthenogenesis reaches up to the crustaceans. . . . (1)

Postulating a belief in "parthogenesis," Diner continues to assert that

> [w]oman, then, created man, not the other way around. She is the postulate, he is the creature; she is the cause, he is the effect. In the guise of the mother she anticipates him, rises up from primeval world spaces up into the personal stratum of individual existence. The deepest sensitivity does not bear the imprint of a father, because fathers at the beginning of consciousness were only brothers. (1-2)

Diner traces the relation between animism and immaculate conception to the Indo-Europeans. She explains that the Vedic nature religion upholds the goddess

Vac as the creative principle, where "*Vac* means language. She is not the male sacred spirit, which disgorges itself through the usual 'fiery tongues'; rather, she is the maternal mouth cavity which forms and awakens the living word without being touched by a tongue as paternal phallus" (6). Significantly, Diner, whose real name is Bertha Eckstein-Diener, published some of her most controversial literature between 1929 and 1940, in Germany, under the pseudonym of Sir Galahad. Diner's personal life, no doubt, crystallized her ideas about the blasphemous association between creation through the written word and the Word of God—a relation that was often punishable under law. Though Lawrence became familiar with ideas similar to Diner's—such as J. J. Bachofen's views on matriarchal values—through his wife, Frieda (Storch 97), such mythic approaches to matriarchy as Diner's and Bachofen's have been caught in much critical cross-fire, accused of being pseudo-scientific and over-simplistic.[79] Today, a much more persuasive approach to matriarchy is taken by Evelyn Acworth in *The New Matriarchy*, which traces matriarchy and patriarchy as family and culture systems that arise out of the needs of historical periods.

The matriarchy that Lawrence presents under the mater's law is ridiculous and dreadful, however, rather than a system to be emulated when useful. We can better understand his presentation in the light of Diane Bornstein's discussion on the representation of women in medieval allegories in her book *The Lady in the Tower*. In these allegories, Bornstein explains, various undesirable traits were stereotypically presented as ugly old women while beautiful young girls represented various desirable traits. Bornstein asserts that the repulsive old woman especially has represented a stereotype in anti-feminist literature where she is portrayed as sexually aggressive, as vitriolic, as a husband hunter or husband tamer, or as vindictive toward the male (10-11). I believe that the female characters in *The Virgin and the Gipsy* are presented in similar ways: the young and attractive Yvette is set up as a contrast to the desiccated Aunt Cissie and the ugly, aging grandmother. Such a contrast calls upon stereotypical associations to make a judgement of the characters and action.

Following Holbrook, I too believe that the satire and comedy surrounding Aunt Cissie and the mater is affected by "too much hostility" (109). The mater's mouth, and therefore her speech, are not venerable. Rather, her mouth is repeatedly referred to as "toad-like," "prognathous," and "trap-like" (*The Virgin and the Gipsy* 537). Like a trap, her speech inhibits her children and grandchildren and drives them to be secretive. By extension, like the mater's mouth, the rectory—the mater's stronghold, where the windows are always kept shut—traps its inhabitants, takes their freedom, and is represented as a symbol of a life lived indoors. The inhibited existence of the inmates of the rectory is in sharp contrast to the gipsy's life of freedom. It is understandable, therefore, for Yvette to desire to "live in a camp, in a caravan, and never set foot in a house, not know the existence of a parish, never look at a church. . . . She hate[s] the rectory and everything it implie[s]" (499). Later, when the gipsy visits Yvette's house to sell his wares, he busies "himself at his cart *outside* the white gate, with that air of silent and forever-unyielding *outsideness* . . . [and] he str[ikes] stealthily at the *inside* of the establishment. . . . But she [is] born *inside* the pale" (my italics 538-9).[80] The tension between the inside and outside manifests Yvette's inner struggle, torn between her own and the gipsy's way of life. Yvette is repulsed by her own environment and is enormously attracted to the gipsy's freedom, for "if she belonged to any side, and to any clan, it was to his" (539); yet she is unable to relinquish the pleasure and the prestige of being a rector's daughter, for "[s]he want[s] to be safe under the temple roof" (539).

Appropriately, in this tale about freedom and its assertion, speech and its lack, or insane utterances, serve an important symbolic function. In this tale, speech incorporates all the edicts—such as those of the patriarchal and the matriarchal law—within which this family operates. As a rector, Mr. Saywell is the symbol of patriarchal law. His speech, appropriately, represents both secular and religious law. In his house, the younger females are constantly told what to do. The mater asks them to deliver redundant messages, Aunt Cissie scolds and punishes them for rudeness to the mater, and the rector lectures Yvette on her irresponsible behavior with the church fund, and later asks her to choose between staying within the purity of his household or being around degenerates like the Eastwoods. Not only does the mater form part of the rector's household, but her utterances represent matriarchal law that parallels the law of the rector. Having slept with her husband for fifty-four years and had six children by him, she is in charge of her granddaughters' moral upbringing, and exercises control over all her children. Lawrence's narrator tells us that "this old woman ha[s] a cunning heart, seeking for ever her own *female power*. And through the weakness of the unfresh, stagnant men that *she ha[s] bred, she ke[eps] her power*" (my italics 475). The mater's power is also represented through the nightly "game" she plays with her two sons. On the one hand, the routine crossword puzzle emphasizes her increasing deafness; on the other hand, it also suggests the lack of communication in this house—a lack that is based on more than a physical disability. This lack of communication implies a split between speech and action in the family that John Turner correctly reads as proof of the fact that "the Saywells are not the Do-wells" (147).

The debilitating effect of the mater's power is most evident in her relation with her grown unmarried daughter, Cissie.[81] The mater's speech/law successfully prevents Aunt Cissie from expressing her sexuality. For instance, because the mater has never slept alone, she must have a sleeping companion. Since even at the age of forty Aunt Cissie has no companion of her own to sleep with, she is the mater's obvious choice. Significantly, though Aunt Cissie's lack of sexual life becomes the reason for her being the mater's choice of bed-companion, the mater thus also ensures Aunt Cissie's chastity. Though the mater is happy with the results, her daughter becomes increasingly bitter. In brief, the narrator tells us that though Aunt Cissie hates the idea of serving as companion to her mother, she complies. But as time passes, Aunt Cissie loses sleep, becomes "greyer and greyer, and the food in the house . . . [gets] worse, and . . . [she has] to have an operation" (*The Virgin and the Gipsy* 481). Aunt Cissie, like all other people in the family, is aware of having devoted her life to her mother, and now she can do nothing but pray about her situation. Now, the "poor thing . . . cease[s] to be Cissie, [for] she ha[s] lost her life and her sex," says Lawrence (475). Further, as she "creep[s] towards fifty, strange green *flares of rage* . . . come up in her, and at such times, she [is] *insane*" (my italics 475). Lawrence's presentation of Aunt Cissie's fits of rage suggesting her insanity are in feminist terms her attempts to articulate her rebellion against the matriarchal law.[82]

Aunt Cissie's increasing spates of insanity are especially apparent in relation to Yvette and Lucille, whose youth and carefree behavior emphasize her own lacks. Even after the fracas over Yvette's appropriation of the church funds has been settled by the rector, Aunt Cissie bursts into Yvette's room to scream at her. "'Liar! Thief! Selfish little beast' *hissed* the *maniacal face* of Aunt Cissie," the narrator tells us (my italics 498). Yvette wants to scream back, but she is silenced when Aunt Cissie shuts the door. Later, when Lucille stands up against the mater in defense of her mother, Aunt Cissie orders her upstairs. It is clear that the mater is aware of her effect on her daughter, but she chooses to ignore it.

"Aunt Cissie's life had been sacrificed to the Mater, and Aunt Cissie knew it, and the Mater knew she knew it" (474). Unable to break away from the mater herself, Aunt Cissie perpetuates the mater's rule. Thus, Aunt Cissie's unmarried state is clearly established as the reason for her dementia.

Just as the mater's mouth—the source of her speech, and by extension, her law—controls Aunt Cissie's sexuality and leads to her insane behavior, Aunt Cissie's own mouth also serves as a rich symbol in this tale. The mouth is most obviously associated with food. Discussing "the symbolic value of food," Turner says that "food brings the comfort to the body that love and affection bring to the mind, whilst the shared experience of eating reinforces the individual's bond to his social group" (148-9). But the mouth may also be associated with other kinds of appetite. In the tale, the only two people who eat with any gusto are the mater and the rector. The other members of the Saywell household merely pick at their food. Aunt Cissie, in particular, doesn't like to eat her meals. She rejects, that is, all that food symbolizes.

In contemporary terms, Aunt Cissie's food habits and general behavior recreate a troubling vision of anorexic behavior which is primarily a woman-centered eating disorder. Joan Jacobs Brumberg, in her historical look at this disorder, traces its place in Victorian society. In the chapter, "The Appetite as Voice," she refers to the association between food and femininity during those times. Not only was food choice considered "a form of self-expression," but "[d]isplays of appetite were particularly difficult for young women who understood appetite to be both a sign of sexuality and an indication of lack of self-restraint" (178). In documented cases of its treatment, the (male) physician—looking for overt symptoms—would often turn to the parent, especially the mother, to discuss the issue; thus, relegating the patient to the status of a child. Brumberg refers to specific cases where the patient who was silent in front of the doctor would often discuss her concerns with a subordinate at the hospital. Moreover, the patient may engage in undercover relations with other patients to get hold of food to eat on the sly (169-70). Emphasizing the sex segregated world of the Victorians where discussion of female issues with males was often taboo, Brumberg asserts that "[t]he silence of the Victorian anorectic was in keeping with her provocative resort to symbolic rather than rhetorical behavior" (171).

Medical and psychological studies such as those of Paul Garfinkel and David Garner (1982) that demonstrate the relation of anorexic behavior to "concerns with control over one's life, identity, autonomy, self-worth, and bodily preoccupations" (33) within the female are now fairly common. Among other things, Garfinkel and Garner point out that often there are "disturbed parent-child relationships in families with an anorexic individual" (177). While they admit that these family relationships can fall into various patterns, they refer to V. Szyrynski's study (1973) that states: "[In such families, d]omestic life is dominated by the mother, with a rather passive and ineffectual father in the background" (177). A spotlight on anorexic behavior thus allows us to read Aunt Cissie's character as one who tries to assert some form of control in her life by constantly punishing her own body or her nieces; it also points a finger of blame at the repressive and authoritarian forces in society that provoke such behaviors.

More conventionally, the text suggests that Aunt Cissie's rejection of ordinary food indicates her fear of sex. But she continues to stuff her mouth with chocolates, which, together with her reaction to the gipsy, may hint at her openness to seduction. When the gipsy comes to the rectory door to see Yvette, he successfully induces Aunt Cissie to buy his wares by adopting a tender and submissive tone. "Aunt Cissie saw how handsome he was, saw the flexible curve of his lips under the line of black moustache, and she was fluttered," says the narrator (*The Virgin and the Gipsy* 508). This episode not merely serves to establish banked and frustrated desire within Aunt Cissie, but also puts into perspective the much younger Yvette's reaction to the gipsy.

In fact, the numerous discussions in this tale about appetite and desire serve as propaganda to justify Yvette's passion for the gipsy. But though the text makes abundant provision for justifying Yvette's response to the gipsy, the narrative also suggests that all female behavior in the tale is finally deviant. The text justifies Yvette's passion for the gipsy when Major Eastwood tells Yvette and the Jewess that "desire is the most wonderful thing in life" (531). When the Jewess objects and calls it the most common of sentiments, the Major disagrees and differentiates between the common man's appetite and the "rich man's" desire. But the text also portrays female behavior as deviant, as a kind of enactment of Foucault's belief that the bourgeois world after 1650 has circumscribed "all deviant and oppositional behaviour under the taboos of prison or madhouse, and of the consequent impoverishment of language and imagery" (quoted in Turner 150-51). In the beginning, Cynthia's elopement with the young man is described as a "touch of madness" (*The Virgin and the Gipsy* 471). Later, the rector threatens Yvette with the lunatic asylum if she does not control her degeneracy in meeting the Eastwoods. On the other hand, Aunt Cissie has grown into a lunatic in a rectory that offers no asylum, substantiating Becker's reference to the "life-denying atmosphere [of the rectory], which has already dried up . . . Aunt Cissie" (123). Because the life-affirming examples in this tale are associated with a free expression of one's sexuality, the silence of the text associates virginity with potential insanity. The narrator seems to sanction the madness of Cynthia, of Mrs. Fawcett and of Yvette, but to perceive Aunt Cissie as pitiable.

From the start, both the younger females have the opportunity to choose between a "selfish" way of life as represented by their mother and Mrs. Fawcett and a rigidly principled but lonely life under a matriarchal system as represented by Aunt Cissie. We are told that just as in the beginning Mrs. Arthur Saywell ("She-who-was-Cynthia"), the Vicar's wife, leaves behind her husband and two young children to be with the man she loves, so does Mrs. Fawcett, the young Jewess, leave behind her two young children to be with Mr. Eastwood, her lover. This parallels Lawrence's life with Frieda (Tedlock 206, Holbrook 113), and it also parallels Mrs. Fawcett and the Jewess, in "The Last Laugh," who welcomes Marchbanks in the anticipation of something wonderful. All these relationships are presented as life-affirming in Lawrence's fiction.

The text portrays Yvette's "madness" as sympathetically as that of her mother and Mrs. Fawcett. But initially, by defining her beauty, like that of Winifred in "The Witch a la Mode," as mesmeric and seductive, the narrator evokes the association between beauty and bewitchery. For example, Yvette's "sensitive nose turned up, [and] her soft brown hair fell like a soft sheath round her tender, flower-like face, as she sat musing," says Lawrence (*The Virgin and the Gipsy* 514). By describing Yvette in this manner, Lawrence appears to suggest that her physical beauty attracts and indeed compels the gipsy to seduce her. But we are also informed that the more housetrained of the males such as Leo, though *afraid* of her power, pursue her as well (514). Just as the gipsy disregards his wife and five children to pursue Yvette, so does Leo disregard Ella, the woman to whom he is practically engaged, to pursue Yvette. This association between the gipsy and Leo, which is emphasized when Yvette is described as a "virgin witch" (514), makes us question the fittingness of establishing the gipsy as an outsider to Yvette's world. Describing her both as a "Lady of Shallott" (505) and a "witch" (493, 514),[83] the narrator once again evokes the tension between the gipsy's and Yvette's ways of life. For Yvette can not be both a part of the establishment and therefore an insider and also a witch and therefore an outsider.

The narrator repeats his complex portrayal of Yvette in the final scene of the tale when he suggests that like the sleeping beauty, Yvette, too, is transformed by her experience with the gipsy (552). To understand the significance of this tale and especially the final scene, we must read transformations in fairy tales, like Hedwig Von Beit in "The Problem of Transformation in the Fairy Tale," as "a mirroring of a process of the psyche" (57). Though readings of this tale as a fairy-tale—especially in association with the sleeping beauty story—are fairly common (Ford 101, Moore 393), Holbrook counters romantic readings such as that of F. R. Leavis, who reads this tale as "a tenderly reverend study of virginal young life" (quoted in Holbrook 112). For Holbrook, Yvette

> is in a state of revolt from her family, while the gypsy is seeking to seduce her partly as a gesture of defiance and challenge to established society: "his race was very old, in its peculiar battle with established society, and had no conception of winning. Only now and then could it score." (106)

In response to Leavis, Holbrook asserts that the tale's emphasis is on the gipsy's plotting to get Yvette. He analyses the final act of copulation between Yvette and the gipsy, not as a regenerative experience of love, but, in fact, as a one-night stand and a possibly painful experience for a young virgin suffering from shock and fear—an experience that could leave lasting damage on the emotional well-being of a young girl. Consequently, he interprets Yvette's longing for the gipsy as the result of youthful idolization (110-14). John Humma continues this line of interpretation when he reads at least "a tinge of irony" in the gipsy's letter to Yvette where he signs himself her "obdt. servant" (*The Virgin and the Gipsy* 553) after his proven mastery in their common experience (Humma 79).

Such readings as those of Holbrook and of Humma, by stressing the pariah-like nature of the gipsy, have shifted the critical focus from its previous emphasis on regeneration in this tale to youthful indiscretion. Holbrook and Humma are correct that to be another Aunt Cissie may not be desirable, but a single experience with the gipsy is no answer to the problem of boredom that Yvette encounters on her return from finishing school. Lawrence tells us that in the beginning, on their return from school, both Yvette and Lucille are faced with boredom and the example of their Aunt Cissie. No amount of charity work or family obligations has been able to eliminate Aunt Cissie's loneliness. Her "madness" is doubly problematic as it implicates the prohibitive nature of all "systems of law"—matriarchal or patriarchal. While Lucille counters her problem of boredom by at least committing herself to some work, Yvette finds herself attracted to the gipsy despite the fact that she consciously recognizes her own difference from him (*The Virgin and the Gipsy* 538-39). Not only does she keep her meeting with him a secret from her family, but she also consummates her passion for him only under under a semi-conscious state of fear and shock. As a result, the action suggests that it is not a wilfully sought and desired mating; she merely submits to circumstance. It would therefore be inappropriate to term her one experience with the gipsy as an experience of love.

Though feminists such as Helene Cixous and Luce Irigaray celebrate the female body as an expression of female experience, I do not believe that a mere expression of sexuality—as Yvette's in the tale—out of the context within which it occurs necessarily expresses liberation. Though Yvette expresses pity for the "old maids" who are possibly thinking of falling in love and getting married and wonders why they care and even rejects Leo's proposal made with the threat of her turning into an old maid, she does no more than cursorily agree with Lucille that they should have fun with the males who are "decent" to them. Lawrence thus suggests here that Yvette responds to more than sexual desire when she responds to the gipsy. Yet when she sees the "shadows under poor Lucille's eyes, and the wistfulness in the beautiful eyes themselves," she wishes that "some awfully nice, kind, protective sort of man would but marry [Lucille]" (528). This desire in Yvette to find someone for Lucille suggests the possibility of a similar desire for herself. Therefore, when we imbue Yvette's sexual initiation with spiritual meaning, we do so at the expense of Aunt Cissie's lack of sexual life. Such a comparison is both inappropriate and unnecessarily cruel to Aunt Cissie's character, for it validates sexual experience (even under questionable circumstances) over celibacy.

By implication, exalting Yvette's experience with the gipsy also validates the heterosexual relation as that without which a woman can only be a desiccated "old maid." For example, when Yvette voices her belief in the innocence of the Eastwoods, her father, the rector, threatens her with "a criminal-lunacy asylum" (534). She soon comes to doubt that she is perhaps one of the criminally lunatic. Thus, in *The Virgin and the Gipsy* Lawrence uses the confrontation between Aunt Cissie's way of life and that of Yvette to suggest the increasing need to repulse all forms of organized and structured society. By depicting Yvette as struggling against her natural desires, Lawrence also suggests his own continuing unresolved feelings over this issue.[84] But most of all, though Lawrence portrays Yvette as sexually liberated and Aunt Cissie as verbally articulate, he yet captures the debilitating impact of both matriarchy and patriarchy—systems that necessitate Yvette's hiding her experience from others and that merely ridicule Aunt Cissie's spurts of expression as meaningless.

IV

Written in two parts, from 1927 to 1928, *The Escaped Cock* is a tale that conflates Christian and pagan myth.[85] Its third part exists in the form of an essay, "The Risen Lord," written in 1929, and published posthumously in *Phoenix II*. Briefly, this tale, which is otherwise known as *The Man Who* Died, is about the resurrection of Christ.[86] In the beginning, we are told that a peasant near Jerusalem has a beautiful cock. Though the cock is good as a rooster, he's easily lured by the calls of other cocks. Therefore, the peasant keeps the cock tethered to prevent it from escaping.

But one day the cock escapes. This very same day, Christ, the man who had died, rises. The peasant gives him shelter, for he knows that otherwise the people would betray him again. At this time, since the man has not yet ascended to the Father, he can not bear to be touched by humans and *noli me tangere* becomes his constant refrain. Thus, when a young female, Madeleine, offers him money, he refuses her by telling her that he does not want any contact. Another reason why he abhors contact with Madeleine is that he can see that just as in the past she was guilty of taking too much from others, now she is guilty of committing another kind of excess—that of wanting to give too much. Since he believes that too much giving is as wrong as too much taking in a relationship, he gives

Madeleine's money to the peasant's wife. But when the latter tries to reciprocate this good turn by offering him her body, the risen man declines her offer. He leaves after buying the cock. On the way, he enters his cock in a cock fight. But when his cock wins, he turns him over to the loser, and proceeds on his journey. Finally, he arrives at the house of a priestess, the woman of Isis. The narrator informs us that she is as glad to see the risen man as he is to see her because she has been searching for him. She feels "in the quick of her soul" that this is her lost Osiris (585). Both searches end when man and woman consummate their passion. While she heals him with her touch, he impregnates her. But not wanting any betrayers to catch him, after they make love, he prepares to leave with a promise to return.

This promise is fulfilled in "The Risen Lord." This essay offers Lawrence's harangue about the incomplete truth that churches preach. He asserts that churches must preach not only about Christ's birth and his crucifixion, but also his resurrection. By not preaching about the resurrection, the churches rob the people of the fruitfulness it represents. Lawrence reminds the people that among other images the Catholic church has given to the world images of the Christ-child and Christ-crucified. The one prepares us for the other. Yet, says Lawrence, many people refuse to follow the progression. He reminds us that the image of the woman as a Madonna-like figure and a shelter of peace was shattered by World War I. Making an association between the soldier at war and the crucified Christ, Lawrence defines the soldier's position as essentially womanless. But since the women largely remained outside the war experience, they continued to hold on to their pre-war image of themselves. Lawrence doubts that the Protestant churches, who supported the war, will ever preach about the resurrected Christ—though the Catholic church may. Lawrence digresses here briefly and refers to the practices of the Mediterranean countries where Easter is the biggest holiday, and the myths of Adonis and Christ are conflated to celebrate the new year. Since Easter celebrates the resurrection, Lawrence asserts that as Christians "we rise with Him in the body" (574). To understand and appreciate the full significance of the resurrection, says Lawrence, we must understand that not only did Christ rise from the dead, but he rose to full physical being. This means that he rose to work, to be with a woman, and to have children with her. The risen lord also rose to continue his earlier battles and to defeat Satan. If approached again by Satan, this time he would deny the promise of power in the temptations and refuse crucifixion because the real power lies in life itself and in having risen again.[87]

Though Lawrence was fascinated with Christ's resurrection, he had an unconventional interest in it. Earl Brewster notes his account of the conception of the idea for *The Escaped Cock*:

> My memory is that Easter morning found us at Grosseto [in fact Volterra]: there we passed a little shop, in the window of which was a toy rooster escaping from an egg. I remarked that it suggested a title—*The Escaped Cock*—a story of the Resurrection. Lawrence replied that he had been thinking about writing a story of the Resurrection: later in the book of that title which he gave to me, he has written: "I've been doing a story of the Resurrection—what sort of a man 'rose up,' after all that other pretty little experience. Rather devastating." (quoted in Sagar, *D.H.Lawrence: A Calendar of his Works* 160)[88]

Writing to the Brewsters on May 3, 1927, Lawrence himself admitted his new interest in the idea of the resurrection. He said:

> I wrote a story of the Resurrection, where Jesus gets up and feels very sick about everything, and can't stand the old crowd any more—so cuts out—and as he heals up, he begins to find what an astonishing place the phenomenal world is, far more marvellous than any salvation or heaven—and thanks his stars he needn't have a "mission" any more. (*Collected Letters* II 975)[89]

But Lawrence's celebration of the resurrection of Christ is defiant in spirit. Indeed, in a letter to Curtis Brown, Lawrence wrote that if Spud Johnson didn't publish *The Escaped Cock* he would "write a second half to it—the phallic second half [he] always intended to add to it" (quoted in Sagar, *D.H. Lawrence: A Calendar of his Works* 171). We must also remember that Lawrence wrote *The Escaped Cock* at the same time as he wrote *Lady Chatterley's Lover*, a novel that unquestionably celebrates phallic love. Since celebrating Christ's purity would suggest a celebration of sterility, a position that is diametrically opposed to

Lawrence's ideology of love in fiction, in "The Risen Lord" he, therefore, celebrates the rebirth of Christ's physical being. But because of Lawrence's assertions about such progressive ideas, he has often been accused of blasphemy (Becker 124, Moore 443-5). Some of his blasphemous statements, for example, were made as early as 1912. Lawrence had written to Edward Garnett that "Christ on the cross must have hated his countrymen. . . . God, how I hate them—I nauseate—they stink in sourness" (*Collected Letters* I 134). Later, in 1914, he was to write to Gordon Campbell that "[i]n the medieval period, Christianity did *not* insist on the Cross: but on the Resurrection . . . . Now . . . [w]e are too mean to get any further" (*Collected Letters* I 301).

With *The Escaped Cock*, Lawrence tried to get further. His effort focuses on his representations of unmarried female characters. In this tale, Lawrence portrays three images of unmarried women: Madeleine, the young female slave, and the woman of Isis. In the first episode, he presents the risen man's encounter with Madeleine, the ex-prostitute. In this brief sketch we learn that in the past, as a prostitute, Madeleine has been guilty of being selfish and grasping. She took more than she gave. Now, wanting to turn over a new leaf, she is guilty of being "selfish" in another way by being too giving. The "need for excessive giving was in her, and she could not bear to be denied," says the narrator (565). The risen man recognizes this need in Madeleine. He recognizes that a "cloud of necessity [is] on her, to be saved from the old, wilful Eve, who had embraced many men, and taken more than she gave." He understands that now "the other doom [is] on her. She want[s] to give without taking" (565-66). By presenting Madeleine as a composite of two extremes, Lawrence repeats his earlier presentation of women (such as in "The Christening") as both the madonna and the whore, the polarities within which culture has locked women, and takes it a step further. He also appears to suggest that both these positions are inappropriate. As a consequence, when the risen man rejects monetary help from Madeleine, the action suggests he supports the need for women to stand up for themselves and assume their rightful place in society. But in order to appreciate the validity of this position, we also need to study the two other portrayals of unmarried women in this tale.

The second image of unmarried women that Lawrence portrays is that of the young female slave brutally raped by a male slave.[90] According to the tale, when one of the pigeons that the slaves had been sacrificing escapes, the seventeen-year-old male slave turns in anger to the young female. Seizing her "in an access of rage," he "beat[s] her with his fist that was stained with pigeon's blood" (576). The female slave, in response, lies on the floor, quivering. After the boy ceases to beat her, he crouches over her "touching her, trying to make her speak" (576). When the female slave continues to lie inert—though "there is fight in her shoulders"—the male slave gets desperate, grabs her by the hips and consummates his passion. Having satisfied himself, he becomes aware of his mistress watching them and scuttles away. But when the female slave looks up, she sullenly turns away and continues her previous chore of stripping the pigeons of their feathers. In feminist terms, this scene of sado-masochistic passion portrays a picture of tortured sexuality in the young female slave. Because within the patriarchy women's sexuality was repressed, or silenced, dreams of rape often served as a means of expressing female sexual desire. Such dreams suggest that though the patriarchy may consider the *expression* of sexual desire in women unnatural and unfeminine, women do experience such desire. But in contrast to his previous fictions such as "You Touched Me" and *The Fox*, Lawrence does not use dreams as a means of expressing sexual desire in this tale. He dramatizes desire in the female slave by emphasizing that though she was inert in the arms of the male slave when "he put his arms round her and lifted her," yet "she slipped back to earth [as if] dead . . . [but] far too quick for anything dead" (576). Moreover, when the male slave holds her firmly at the hips, though "*[t]here* she seem[s] inert, all her fight is in her shoulders" (my italics 576). The female slave's inert lower body contradicts the quickness of life in her upper body and thus suggests in terms of classical psychology the woman's desire to abdicate responsibility from participation in sexual activity.

Studies on rape by feminists such as Susan Brownmiller (1975) and Andrea Dworkin (1989) warn us that such depictions of internal divisiveness within the female regarding issues of sexuality are harmful to women. They misrepresent rape as a healthy sexual act or a crime of passion, as well as an act in which the woman is secretly an accomplice to her own humiliation and torture. They also abdicate responsibility of the male. They describe these representations as pornography and portraits of hatred toward women that have shaped gender relations in culture. While I agree with the need to take seriously the issue of pornography (which continues to be woman-centered) and the definition of rape as a sexual crime of power, I do not believe that all (depictions of) sexual acts (even those that are sado-masochistic) are at all times crimes committed by men on women. Such a definition merely duplicates patriarchal attitudes by, among other things, not allowing individual women to make their own sexual choices—however deviant these may be from the norm. More than that, I believe that the strategic placement of this image—*imbedded* between the first and third images of transformations—is key to our interpretation of it. In fact, it leads to the image of the final union.

The woman of Isis waiting for union with the risen man is Lawrence's third image of unmarried women in this tale. With this image of a woman whose sexuality is more participatory, Lawrence tries to offset the vision of violent passion in the previous image. Now Lawrence compares the experience of the slaves who participate in a sado-masochistic passion with the experience of the priestess and the man who share a healing passion. Referring to the expression of contempt with which the priestess dismisses the slaves: "Slaves! Let the overseer watch them. She was not interested" (577), Harris interprets this scene as not merely representative of a cultural fact, but also as indicative of the man and the priestess's inhuman aloofness from the common experience. She believes that the tenderness the priestess and the risen man share is diminished by their attitude toward the slaves, for they show a blindness, rather than an awakening, to the phenomenal world (242-3).

Though Harris's observations are astute, I believe that the focus of this tale is on the presentation of the *difference* between the two experiences—that between the two slaves and that between the risen man and the priestess. Critics such as Monroe Engel, R. P. Draper, and David Holbrook discuss Lawrence's juxtaposition of the two experiences. While Engel discusses the juxtaposition as a difference between the sexuality that is evoked between the man and the priestess and that between the slaves (the latter is described as more brutal and animalistic [99]), Draper asserts that the different portrayals of the two sexual experiences represent the risen man's rebirth "into an awareness of the phenomenal world, not into an illusion that it is perfect and beautiful and innocent" (147). Holbrook extends Draper's argument when he says that the difference in the two forms of sexuality portrays the man-who-died's realization that such is the common herd of humanity for whom he sacrificed himself (134). These critics are correct. By setting up this difference in the two forms of sexuality, Lawrence sets up a difference between the two principles of give and take. While he suggests that the sexual act of the slaves (the male in particular) represents selfishness and inconsideration, he also suggests that we can find a more balanced relation between the other couple.

But a point of contention in this tale is the way in which the man acquires the priestess. Both Widmer and Holbrook assert that one should not sentimentalize Lawrencean eros in the story (Widmer 210, Holbrook 135). Holbrook agrees with Widmer's opinion that the man gains the priestess through fraud. Further, Holbrook traces a parallel between the gipsy's seduction of the virgin in *The Virgin and the Gipsy* and the man's copulation with the priestess in *The Escaped Cock*. Since both are isolated experiences, he reads them both as one-night stands that merely celebrate "penis-ecstasy" (135). The parallel between these two tales is especially clear when we remember that Yvette, in *The Virgin and the Gipsy*, equates her refusal of the gipsy to Peter's betrayal of Christ before the cock's third crow.

Many critics have trouble accepting Lawrence's religious vision.[91] But my focus in this tale is not on the fact that the risen man and the woman of Isis do not remain together (in the short novel), that is, on the nature of the risen man's experience; rather, it is on the symbolic significance of the act of the resurrection. If we move from the literal to the symbolic, we will then see the risen lord not merely as the embodiment of the male, but, through the experience of the resurrection, as the embodiment of both the female and the male. For within the context of the tale the resurrection serves as a metamorphic event. When Lawrence had earlier tried to introduce the idea of metamorphosis in terms of a secular relationship in *The Virgin and the Gipsy*, his experiment had been limited in scope and vision. Thus, while we can appreciate the change within Yvette after her experience with the gipsy, it is more difficult for us to accord this experience the stature of spiritual ecstacy. The limitation in vision in that tale had therefore resulted from the inefficacy of the intensity of the religious symbolism in relation to human experience. With *The Escaped Cock* Lawrence was to be more successful, for the risen lord, or Christ, is both a man and a myth; he has a real and mythic past. A very tenuous thread—Lawrence's insistent equation of Christ with woman in his fiction—pulls together his religious vision. In "The Overtone," Lawrence explained that Christ dead was woman, Christ risen is man. Lawrence first introduced the idea of the risen lord by referring to Major Eastwood and the gipsy in *The Virgin and the Gipsy* as resurrected men. In that tale, when related to a secular theme, the idea appeared more laughable and pretentious than a vehicle for metaphysical reasoning. By adopting the religious metaphor of the resurrection, Lawrence may be accused of blasphemy by the orthodox, but he is yet able to exploit the metaphor's richness to his advantage.

But even if we accept Lawrence's religious vision, at first the vision of unmarried women that Lawrence presents in this tale appears to be dissatisfying. For, finally, it is a vision that requires heterosexuality for the achievement of human completeness. Lawrence even manipulates the myth of Isis and Osiris to prove the correctness of his vision. Indeed, as Cynthia Lewiecki-Wilson points out, Lawrence significantly leaves out part of the Isis-Osiris myth that informs us of the missing phallus of Osiris. She says that according to Plutarch's account of the myth, "Osiris's body had been scattered in fourteen pieces, [and] she never found the last," though she consecrated the one that was made in imitation (193). We know that Lawrence unashamedly asserted in "The Risen Lord" that if Christ "rises with hands and feet, as Thomas knew for certain: and if with hands and feet, then with lips and stomach and *genitals of a man. Christ risen, and risen in the whole of His flesh, not with some left out*" (my italics 574). Therefore, like Lewiecki-Wilson, I believe that though the man who rises, as Osiris, is dismembered, he rises to take "his place as the inheritor of patriarchal culture" (191).[92] Consequently, he validates his own union with the woman of Isis over that of the young slaves, or that of the transformation of Madeleine from whore to madonna. Lawrence presents the risen man as operating under a patriarchal system wherein it is significant that his own transformations from death to life, from the representative of woman to the representative of man, from the principle of give to the principle of take, are not enough unless they accompany his final heterosexual union.

But this tale more than culminates in Lawrence's portrayal of a successful heterosexual union; it also culminates in Lawrence's exploratory portrayal of images of unmarried women. Though Lawrence portrays the image of the young female slave participating in a sado-masochistic passion, he also constructs two experimental images of unmarried women. The text does not validate Madeleine's transformation, or even that of the risen man himself, but the fact that Lawrence presents such transformations at all is significant. Unlike his ambiguous but conventional portrayal of Emma Rowbotham as a madonna who is perceived as a whore in "The Christening," his portrayal of Madeleine as both a whore and a madonna is much more innovative. In the image of Madeleine, Lawrence shows the possibility of women to will themselves into either polarity. Rather than an either/or, he contemplates the possibility of and/and, or both simultaneously, a decidedly more complex vision of female possibilities. He repeats this possibility in his portrayal of Christ's—and, by extension of his fictional mythology, woman's—resurrection. Further, though Lawrence presents the heterosexual union of the risen man and the woman of Isis as the most desirable union, he portrays the woman of Isis as more independent than any other previous female character in his fiction. By portraying her as seeking the risen man and then greeting him with eagerness, she surpasses the reluctance with which Ursula Brangwen united with Birkin in *Women in Love* (1916) and fulfills the promise that Elsa Laskell makes to herself in "The Overtone" (1924). With the woman of Isis, Lawrence comes closer to portraying a "star-equilibrium" relation—a relation that is perfectly balanced and where both the male and the female are complete in him/herself as well as in conjunction with each other.

***

Though a study of Lawrence's language in the short novels demonstrates that he often perpetuates patriarchal attitudes toward unmarried women, it also reveals his latent feminist concerns. For instance, Lawrence's portrayal of sexuality in unmarried women is more experimental in the short novels than in the short stories. In the short novels, Lawrence tries to implicate both the younger and older female characters in the sexual revolution to explode the idea of women as either madonnas or whores, as figures of the Lady of Shallott or of the witch, and to probe the possibility that women should be conceptualized as both/and. In the past, in stories such as "The Witch a la Mode" and "The Christening," when he had tried to explore these ideas, he had failed. His language in those stories revealed how, and why, patriarchal society continues to frame women within binary positions. But in the short novels, by presenting unmarried women in atypical sexual relations—as the lesbian couple, March and Banford, in *The Fox*—Lawrence appears to explode the binary oppositions within which they have been bound. He takes this experimentation a step further in his portrayal of the transformation of Madeleine from a prostitute to a saint, in

The Escaped Cock. Moreover, in *The Virgin and the Gipsy*, he explores the impact of matriarchy on the sexuality of unmarried women to determine that this system of social organization can be as sexually inhibiting as the patriarchy. Though experimentation does not in itself constitute a challenge to the patriarchy, it does incarnate Lawrence's inner struggle with patriarchal impositions on unmarried women, and his continuing efforts to resolve this struggle within himself.

Chapter 5

Conclusion

It is when one has been able to reach the moment of opening oneself completely to the other that the scene of History will be able to take place in a very vast way.

Helene Cixous

I

Because D. H. Lawrence almost always portrays unmarried women characters in circumstances of defeat—a defeat that may be self-imposed or imposed by the patriarchy—he has often been accused by critics such as Margaret Storch of misogyny and thus of being a descendant of William Blake. Critics also cite his non-fictional writings as further proof of his anti-feminism, if not his misogyny. In agreement with these critics, I believe that Lawrence often expresses his patriarchal beliefs and reservations in much of his fiction and non-fiction. Just as he expresses essentialist attitudes toward women in essays such as "Cocksure Women and Hensure Men," he expresses male chauvinism in other essays. For example, in "Give Her a Pattern" Lawrence expounds on the various images of women in history that men have produced. In this essay, he blames women for wanting a pattern to emulate, and he blames men for not really knowing what they (the men) want. In either case there is chaos, he asserts, because both the men and the women are soon dissatisfied by this state of affairs. Lawrence sees a resolution to this dissatisfaction when men offer women a decent and satisfying pattern to follow (535-38). Though he acknowledges that past patterns of male-female behavior have been dissatisfying for both the females and the males, he expresses his chauvinism by asserting that the men can eliminate the problem between the sexes by providing women with a pattern. Lawrence repeats such chauvinism in his essay “Master in His Own House.” The thrust of this essay lies in his assertion that women are dominant in fields that men no longer care to control. By presenting women’s achievements as the result of men’s lack of interest, he thus undermines the significance of those achievements.

But Lawrence sometimes contradicts these ideas about women and men. This contradiction is evident both in his fiction and non-fiction. For example, when we juxtapose his letter to Katherine Mansfield, in 1918, with his letter to Witter Bynner later in his life, we see that while in 1918 he felt that a woman must yield precedence to a man unquestioningly (*Collected Letters* I 565), later he expressed his boredom with the leader-follower theme in his fiction. He now wanted to express a relation that was more tender and sensitive (*Collected Letters* II 1045). Such contradictions in Lawrence’s discursive prose on the subject of women encourage us to reexamine his positions and to read “between the lines” of his texts for another story to be told.

***

Catherine Belsey and Jane Moore offer us one way to read texts written by male writers such as Lawrence. They emphasize the significance of history to feminism. History, they write,

> provides us with evidence that things have changed. And if they have changed in the past, they do not have to stay as they are now. “Nature,” on the other hand, has long been one of the most powerful weapons in the war against change. If women are passive, helpless and subservient by nature, then feminism is already a lost cause: we shall inevitably revert to type as soon as the present moment of rebellion comes to an end. If men have always been more rational, more judicious, more authoritative, patriarchy is a fact of nature, and women might as well lie back and enjoy it. (3)

But they also assert that feminism has a history. Though we can trace this history back to the seventeenth century, we realize that Lawrence comes at the beginning of the modern movement in feminism traced by Belsey and Moore. Therefore it is important that we understand that though Lawrence frequently illustrates in his short fiction the supremacy of "Nature" in his sometimes essentialist and patriarchal view of unmarried women, in the short fiction he also exhibits his struggle to reexamine and interrogate that position. My study exhibits Lawrence's struggle by reading his texts "against the grain." By challenging the authority of both Lawrence and the critics who continue to read his works in terms of his expressed ideologies, I assert the value of the unsaid over the said to reveal that which was previously concealed. My study thus reveals Lawrence's often unconscious portrayal of images of patriarchy that actually expose not its strengths but the inherent weaknesses of this system of social organization.

The short fiction is replete with assertions and counter-assertions, statements and counter-statements. These contradictions and inconsistencies within Lawrence's fictional and non-fictional positions indicate that because moments of belief may be reversed by another moment, we can not ultimately posit any one of them as false or deceptive. Identity is process for the male as well as the female. Indeed, we may view Lawrence's works as indirect confessions of personal discord or as moments that chart his continual striving to understand "woman." Though such strife within a male writer has been viewed by many feminists as yet further effort of the patriarchy to colonize the female, it is imperative that we not dismiss, because patriarchal, what also asserts the sophistication of Lawrence's artistic position and continues to defy critics' efforts to define it.

II

My study of the short fiction of D. H. Lawrence demonstrates his often contradictory impulse regarding notions of unmarried women and their sexuality. Though Lawrence advocated liberation—of the body—among all classes of women, this liberation was limited primarily to the younger generation. But because Lawrence's images of independence in the younger unmarried women are not celebratory, they undo themselves and point to contradictions within the texts.[93] These contradictions are also evident in his portrayal of the older unmarried women. On the one hand, because he portrays them in typically patriarchal ways in some of his short fiction such as "The Witch a la Mode" (1911-13), "The Christening" (1912), "You Touched Me" (1919), and "Two Blue Birds" (1926), the texts suggest his perpetuation of such stereotypes. On the other hand, because reading "against the grain" reveals his unconscious portrayal of the weakness of patriarchy, or the insidiousness with which patriarchy perpetuates itself, the texts challenge the very stereotypes they appear to perpetuate.

The texts of Lawrence that most apparently challenge the patriarchy are those that exhibit his assertions regarding sisterhood among women. But on this theme, as elsewhere, inconsistency reigns. With *The Fox* (1918-21), Lawrence had introduced the idea of more than friendship between women; he had introduced the idea of a lesbian sexual relation. By depicting unmarried women within this relation, Lawrence tried, without success, to "see" them as functioning outside a heterosexual relation. The text, however, reveals that one of the reasons why the women fail is that though they may share a physical bond, they are not equally committed to their relationship. As a result, Grenfel, like the proverbial fox in a hen-coop, is able to sunder their relation. The text suggests that though Grenfel is physically alone, he draws strength from a bonding with patriarchal belief in the supremacy of the heterosexual over the homosexual. The text thus suggests that the two women might have withstood Grenfel had they had a sense of sisterhood as strong as his patriarchal brotherhood, had they believed in their sexual constitutions as firmly as heterosexual males believe in theirs and its legitimacy.

Lawrence reinforces more overtly his belief in the power of brotherhood and the need for a similar relation among women in "Monkey Nuts" (1919) and "You Touched Me" (1919). In "Monkey Nuts," for example, Lawrence portrays Miss Stokes as an assertive young woman who drives a wagon. Though she tries to take charge of her life by pursuing the young man, Joe, to whom she is attracted, she mortifies him by her blunt efforts. Unable to handle such assertive behavior in a female, with the assistance of his corporal, Albert, and the rest of his male unit, he pushes her away and thus effectively silences her. But though the text overtly depicts male victory, it also reveals that the victory actually conceals defeat, for it shows the patriarchal need to mock—by bonding with other males—that which the patriarchy considers deviant from the norm. Lawrence repeats this self-contradictory image of male comraderie in "You

Touched Me," where the two males, Hadrian and Old Rockley, accomplish the defeat of Emmie and Matilda through complicity with each other and with the help of old laws that favor the patriarchy. These texts, like those others, thus appear to suggest that women, too, could be powerful if they were to bond with each other as, historically, men have done.

With "Tickets, Please" (1918), Lawrence achieves an image—eventually compromised—of sisterhood in his portrayal of young female tram conductors who bond with each other to avenge themselves on the local casanova, John Raynor. When Raynor repeats with Annie his callous behavior with others, she gathers his ex-girlfriends, and they avenge themselves by beating him up and forcing him to choose one of them to marry. Lawrence thus portrays how the collective, in this case the sisterhood, can be a source of strength for any group. But the text also shows that the women's act of revenge is motivated by feelings of disappointment and dismay at not being Raynor's choice. Further, the text reveals that though the women refuse Raynor at the end, they all are unhappy with this choice. The dominant patriarchal system, that is, is finally the best. This ending in many ways echoes the apparently contradictory ending of "Monkey Nuts," where comraderie leads to the public defeat of the identified adversary, but it also signifies the defeat of the individual. Lawrence's texts thus reinforce his belief that when women assume behaviors—such as sisterly bonding—similar to those of men within patriarchy, these behaviors reveal weakness in women as they do that of men in other circumstances.

But with "Two Blue Birds" (1926), Lawrence reverses this theme and returns to his previous concern for a sisterhood among women. By portraying Miss Wrexall as a human echo—a secretary who ignores the truth of the statements of her employer's wife, but regurgitates in triplicate everything her employer dictates—Lawrence suggests that if women are to arm themselves against male exploitation, they need to bond with each other. With this story, Lawrence shifts his view of the dangers of any kind of bonding and returns to his view—previously suggested in *The Fox*—regarding the need for sisterhood among women who hope to overcome patriarchal control.

Lawrence also tries to grapple with patriarchal images of unmarried women as virgins and prostitutes. For example, in "The Witch a la Mode" (1911-13), "You Touched Me" (1919), "The Last Laugh" (1924), "Two Blue Birds" (1926), and *The Virgin and the Gipsy* (1926), Lawrence portrays older unmarried women as "old maids" and "spinsters" who—at best—make good secretaries or teachers, and lack both a sexual existence and a voice. Often the silence to which they are reduced denies them speech and implies their inability to comprehend others. Their apparent inability, which extends to include their sexuality, is suggested by Lawrence's repeated portrayal of them as virgins. Because in his fiction he associates sexual shyness with a shyness about life, he compares these female characters to the "Lady-of-Shallott."[94] Further, because in these instances he associates their attracting men with bewitchery, he suggests they are witches as well. By associating the young and beautiful Winifred Varley in "The Witch a la Mode" and the aristocratic Miss James in "The Last Laugh" with witches,[95] for example, Lawrence informs his presentation of virginity in the female protagonists with a degree of complexity, for in these instances not only does the virginal woman have the power to attract the male, she also has the power to annihilate him. Moreover, a reading "against the grain" reveals two other things: first, it reveals that when the males associate the unmarried females with the Lady of Shallott, they expose their own sexual frustration; second, it reveals that since neither Winifred, in "The Witch a la Mode," nor James, in "The Last Laugh," actively says or does anything to "attract and annihilate" the males, the power they seem to possess comes from the projection of male fantasies. In short, the women are not dangerous in themselves. Just as in "The Witch a la Mode" Coutts's dissatisfaction with his fiancee and his attraction to Winifred is the cause of his being singed by the fire caused by the overturned lamp (a possible metaphor for his attraction to Winifred), so in "The Last Laugh," Marchbanks's own refusal to hear the laugh of Pan (a possible metaphor for communication with the natural spirit) is the cause of his death. Thus, the text reveals both how the patriarchy adopts certain sexist practices such as name-calling to silence women and how the patriarchy's need to resort to such practices reveals its self-destructive weakness.

Lawrence's struggle with patriarchal notions about unmarried women who are also virgins is especially apparent in *The Virgin and the Gipsy*. This text shows not merely how virginity threatens the male but how it also threatens the female—it can make her mad. Though the association between virginity and madness encourages critics to argue that Lawrence perpetuates such patriarchal notions, his text does not "blame" the patriarchy for the creation of this association. Rather, it "blames" the matriarchy. While we could consider it patriarchal of Lawrence to blame the matriarchy, I believe that by showing the inhibiting effect of matriarchy on women, the text also argues the need for a healthy mother-daughter bond among women to counter the impact of the patriarchy.[96] But because Lawrence's sometime struggle against the patriarchy lies concealed in the text, critics continue to overlook its significance.

Lawrence's struggle with patriarchal representations of unmarried women is quite overtly expressed in a story such as "The Christening." As early as 1912, he combines an image of innocence with which he had hitherto associated such women with an image of experience, thus offering patriarchy its deepest challenge in the portrayal of Emma Rowbotham, an ex-miner's daughter, as an unwed mother. In "The Christening," Lawrence shows how the patriarchy often constitutes women in binaries: as a whore or as a madonna. Though Lawrence depicts how patriarchy successfully captures and silences women in both these images, the story also reveals the weakness of a social structure that can survive only by relating to women in uni-dimensional images. The text thus appears to question the image of the woman as either the madonna or the whore. Further, this story marks the beginning of his experimentation with images of unmarried women as prostitutes.

Though Lawrence described prostitution as one of the anti-life institutions in society ("The Risen Lord" 576-77), he also presents some of his strongest images of unmarried women in fiction—such as "The Primrose Path" (1913) and *The Escaped Cock* (1927-28)—that depicts them as prostitutes. "The Primrose Path" suggests that the two unmarried women—the anonymous young female and Elaine—use Sutton, the man they live with, by discarding him and moving on to other men after they have gained materially from him. They thus mimic the stereotypical presentations of men in culture and literature (as, for example, the unknown baker's man in "The Christening" who has an affair with Emma and leaves her pregnant), and appear to uphold his belief that prostitution is indeed one of the anti-life institutions in society. His exploitation of the metaphor of poison in relation to the impact of these two women on Sutton further supports this belief. But the text also reveals that Sutton's bullying attitudes toward women are merely a cover-up for his inherent weakness and inadequacies. Moreover, by emphasizing the youth of the two women and the material advantage that Sutton offers to them, the text suggests that men like Sutton are responsible for prostitution and thus the creation and perpetuation of such institutions.

This ironic image of prostitution paves the way for Lawrence's more apparently positive portrayal of it in *The Escaped Cock.* This tale exploits Biblical symbolism to portray the two extremes of too much giving and too much taking in Madeleine, the ex-prostitute turned saint (Mary Magdalen). Lawrence thus combines here the two images of women with which he appears to have been struggling in his fiction: the madonna and the whore. Because of Lawrence's expressed belief in the heterosexual union[97] and his belief that prostitution is "anti-life," critics continue to ignore what the text reveals about characters such as Madeleine. But I believe that we must re-assess the value of Lawrence's portrayal of the dual transformation: that of Madeleine, and that of the risen man before his union with the woman of Isis. By portraying these two transformations, secular and religious, Lawrence demonstrates the possibility of androgyny.

***

For many people androgyny offers an answer to gender politics. For Carolyn Heilbrun, as for many others, "future salvation lies in a movement away from sexual polarization and the prison of gender toward a world in which individual roles and the modes of personal behavior can be freely chosen" (*Toward a Recognition of Androgyny* xi-xii). The future lies in androgyny. Heilbrun discovered in Plato's *Symposium* the story of circular beings before they were split into males and females. This story traces human history in terms of one half's search for its other half—which may be male or female (xiii). Just as Heilbrun warns against an equation between androgyny and hermaphroditism, Joseph Andriano explains that androgyny is not to be equated with transvestism. To him, androgyny represents a balance, "a surfacing of what was once submerged, a conscious attempt to place masculinity and femininity into a dialectic rather than a hierarchic dualism" (7). Lawrence appears to achieve this symbolic balance between the male and female principles in *The Escaped Cock* by creating, through his dual transformation, the possibility of the androgyne.

The androgyne, as Kari Weil states, "has often been considered to be an archetype or a universal fantasy" (3). Weil explains how "psychoanalysis equates androgyny with a repressed desire to return to the imaginary wholeness and self-sufficiency associated with the pre-Oedipal phase before sexual difference" (3). Because the risen man's later union with the woman of Isis re-establishes sexual difference, and because the transformations within Madeleine and the risen man demonstrate androgyny—what Alexandra Kaplan and Joan Bean describe as "integrative feminine and masculine ways" (2) and what Nancy Downing terms psychological androgyny—the "balance between and the integration of both masculine and feminine characteristics" (quoted in Brandwein 163), I believe we should value Lawrence's portrayal of their transformation as attempts at images of wholeness.

Lawrence first expresses his ideas about androgyny through his portrayal of Madeleine in *The Escaped Cock.* The text reveals that her transformation from whore to saint is similar to that of the risen man's transformation from death to life. The text thus presents in Madeleine an image of the affirmation of life. Therefore, though Lawrence's association of unmarried women with both the Lady of Shallott and prostitutes suggests his perpetuation of cultural stereotypes, his texts often contradict this portrayal and show how these images are products and constructions of the male gaze.

His religious vision repeats the secular experience of Madeleine. Though critics often question whether it is possible to achieve Lawrence's religious vision in reality, two aspects of this vision suggest the possibility of its achievement: first, a belief in Christ's humanity and, second, modern symbolic interpretations of myth that suggest universality of thought in different cultures and ages. In the first instance, to understand Lawrence's portrayal of the popular image from art—of madonna with child—we must realize that the Virgin's humanity assured the humanity of Christ. Margaret Miles, for example, explains how this claim was made by Saint Thomas Aquinas, Tertullian and the Council of Ephesus in 431 A.D., where "Mary was called Theotokos, God-bearer, in order to affirm that Christ, born from her, was true God as well as true man" (200). Lawrence's passionate interest in art suggests his likely acquaintance with this tradition. In the second instance, a symbolic reading of *The Escaped Cock* shows us that the crucified Christ, whom Lawrencean myth equates with the female principle that has prostituted itself by being too giving, is transformed in re-birth into the Pan-like male principle that shall be more of a taker. Like Tiresias, whose lived experience in the body of the female becomes the cause of his later wisdom, the risen man has a past life that makes possible his union with the priestess. Lawrence's career thus reveals that not only does his short fiction portray contradictory images of unmarried women, but it also often presents contradictory themes. His short fiction, moreover, charts no consistent development in his view of unmarried women. In many ways Lawrence's inconsistent images of unmarried women bring to life his complaint, as expressed in his essay "Give Her a Pattern," that women are products of inconsistent male ideas about them. But though these inconsistencies evoke the patriarchy's struggle to come to grips with the idea of what it is to be a woman, he disregards his own ideas in his enactment of them in his fiction. He ends "Give Her a Pattern" by asking men to stop the chaos between women and men by providing women with a "pattern" or image to emulate, but because he associates unmarried women with androgyny in *The Escaped Cock*, we may infer that through this vision he suggests, among other things, the possibility of the greatest autonomy of all for unmarried women—that of being integrated human beings.

III

In Chapter 1 I raised the question of a gender-based determinism of ideas. In this context, we may ask whether it is perhaps indeed Lawrence's gender that is the cause of his frequent perpetuation of patriarchy's images of unmarried women. Lawrence's earlier fictional concerns with the impact of the New Woman on the New Man (to borrow Declan Kiberd's terms) generated a stereotypical male response that eventually gave way to a vision of androgyny—however short-lived it may have been. Lawrence talks about this issue in his essay "On Being a Man." Here, he asserts that the nature of life is such that we "proceed from what we know already to what we know next" (617). But a mere desire to know does not necessarily lead to knowledge. For example, says Lawrence, for him, wanting to know a Negro also constitutes realizing that since he is "not a nigger" he "can't quite know a nigger" or "fully 'understand' him," and that "[k]now thyself means knowing at last that you can't know yourself" (620). But in the essay Lawrence suddenly reverses his position when he says that as human beings the challenge and the adventure of life lie in our willingness to take risks, to go after something despite knowing that it may not lead to what we truly desire. Because life inevitably leads to death we should not prevent ourselves from planting the seeds of new life (621-22).

The expression of such beliefs by Lawrence leads me to disagree with the view that his gender prohibits his participating in the female experience. I disagree with this view especially because I do not believe—as do the proponents of the insider doctrine—that gender differences necessarily prohibit understanding between men and women. Instead, I assert, in agreement with Joseph Allen Boone, that if we expose "the latent multiplicity and difference in the word 'me(n)', we can perhaps open up a space within the discourse of feminism where a male feminist voice can have something to say" and where "his voice may . . . find that it no longer exists as an abstraction" (159). The "issues suffusing the topic of men and feminism should not come to be perceived merely as a set of grammatical relations ('in' or 'for' or 'against')," but should value "the simultaneously lived and practiced dimensions of that relation" (159). Viewing Lawrence in this way, we can see that like other males of his generation he had to acknowledge the changing nature of women's experience and reality and to confront its impact on the male. His fictional concerns are evidence of a lifetime of effort to come to grips with this evolving social phenomenon. Though Lawrence demonstrates his essentialism toward women in his essays and in much of his fiction, I believe his fiction is, foremost, a reaction to the fact that women *do* change. Further, his expressed essentialism is not limited to women; it extends itself to include men. Indeed, it implicates all of human nature. Repeatedly, Lawrence shows in his short fiction that—given the same circumstances and opportunities—the unmarried women will behave in ways similar to those of men. As opposed to those feminists who consider Lawrence's portrayal of women to be limited by his gender, I therefore believe that though Lawrence's inability to portray—unreservedly—an independent unmarried woman may certainly be partly the result of received ideas and his gender construction, his often unwitting portrayal of the insidious impact of patriarchy and his vision of androgyny undercut the attack on his gender-engendered ideas.

***

While feminists have correctly opened up new avenues in literary studies by redefining the canon to include a focus on literature by women, and about women, this new vision is in danger of suffering the limitations of its patriarchal counterpart. Charged with pornography and misogyny, Lawrence has virtually disappeared from the English curriculum at many American campuses. But expungement of material that does not meet the levels of acceptability by some feminists trails behind it a host of other problems. And it naturally follows, therefore, that just as patriarchal attempts to control women's thoughts and actions were unacceptable to women, so are many feminists' attempts to control men's thoughts and actions unacceptable to men. Moreover, because they eliminate freedom of choice from the very women they profess to serve, they contradict the very basis of the feminist movement and are therefore unacceptable to many women who are feminists. What is more valuable is to provide women (and men) with tools to critically analyze such presentations and behavior in order to make more informed individual choices.

Reconstructive studies, such as mine, allow us to see old concepts in new ways. They allow us to see that while the unmarried female characters—the single-most threatening group to the foundation of the patriarchy—in Lawrence's short fiction are constructed in the stereotypical terms of patriarchal language as victims, they are indeed, oftentimes, representatives of strong, independent women. Moreover, such constructions of unmarried women are an integral part of our cultural history from which we have derived, struggling to the present. We need to remember that fact. We also need to recognize that expunging these texts does not eliminate the existence of such attitudes from our collective past or our individual present; they only drive them underground. Thus, creating a false impression in society that such attitudes have indeed been eliminated.

The division among feminists on the issue of pornography repeats the stereotypical constructions/divisions of women by the patriarchy as either/or and continues to resist the notion and rhetoric of being both/and. Resisting the notion and rhetoric of being defined as either moralist or libertarian, I insist on the place and value of both. In the same spirit, I insist on the place and value of Lawrence within the literary canon, especially Women's Studies.

***

Like studies in psychology that value the power of the unconscious, my study of Lawrence also values his silences. Because of his struggle with the images of women as virgins and prostitutes, his advocacy of sisterhood among women and of androgyny—despite his often overt perpetuation of patriarchy—Lawrence overcomes what Mary Gordon describes as Virginia Woolf's frustration with the limitations of modern women and men in transmitting "reality" that prevent literature from being complete (in Woolf xii). By exhibiting an insight into patriarchy as well as into the plight of unmarried women, the Lawrencean text exhibits Lawrence's ability to be "androgynous in mind," thus preventing literature from being incomplete and "permanently flawed" (xii).

Endnotes

Chapter 1

1. All three essays, "Matriarchy," "Cocksure Women and Hensure Men," and "Do Women Change?" were written within a month of each other in 1928, and chart Lawrence's exploratory interest in "woman" during this time.

2. Though I do not discuss here Lawrence's vision of unmarried women in the longer fiction, I believe that in those works Lawrence can "see" his women characters only in relation to the male characters. In the following pages I further discuss this idea in relation to the unmarried women in the short fiction.

3. Lawrence also deals with homoerotic relations between men, as in *Sons and Lovers* and *Women in Love*, but the male discourse in terms of their relationship as well as in terms of Lawrence's attitude and presentation of this relationship, is different from the female discourse. See Barbara Hardy's essay, "Women in D. H. Lawrence's Works" (90-121), and Jeffrey Meyers' essay, "D. H. Lawrence and Homosexuality" (135-46).

In my study, I include Christ, the man who died, in *The Escaped Cock*, among the unmarried female characters. I base my inclusion of Christ in this category on Lawrence's professed association between Christ and the female principle. This association is most clearly articulated in his short story "The Overtone."

4. For instance, Keith Sagar discusses critically the "star polarity" achieved by Ursula and Birkin in *Women in Love* in terms of Lawrence's heroic attempt to see "modern life as it is" (*D. H. Lawrence: Life into Art* 147-93). But James C. Cowan boldly asserts that Lawrence does not advocate blood consciousness over mind consciousness, and demonstrates how, in fact, each extreme leads to the loss of "integral being" (66-67).

5. There are a few unpublished dissertations on Lawrence's shorter fiction. They focus on questions of structure and chronology in Lawrence's art.

6. See Toril Moi's *Sexual/Textual Politics* for a critical perspective on this theory (75-79).

7. Refer to Robin Lakoff's landmark study on women's speech, *Language and Woman's Place.* Its cover design illustrates Lakoff's themes. It shows us, as Allette Olin Hill tells us, "a woman's face with a band-aid covering her mouth; her large expressive eyes look troubled. The message is clear: women have been gagged" (1).

8. Not only have women been objectified and fragmented as sexual beings in art and history, but they have also been denied the life of the intellect. Dale Spender, like Virginia Woolf, deplores the loss of women's intellectual being. She sees this loss as a leading cause for the non-existence of women in culture and literature. Further, Spender agrees with Catherine Mackinnon's study that sees sexual harrassment of women in the work place as a means to keep women in their place (240-30). Spender traces this pattern of harrassment back to the seventeenth century.

9. The older unmarried women in Lawrence's longer fiction, such as Gudrun Brangwen and Hermione Roddice in *Women in Love*, are portrayed as sexually active. Because both these women, however, are presented as "head conscious," they have often been perceived as ridiculous by critics. While both

are outspoken and actively assert themselves, their choices are presented as less significant than the choices of a woman such as Ursula Brangwen, who achieves apparent harmony (or "star equilibrium") in her marriage to Birkin.

10. Refer to Betty Friedan's *The Feminine Mystique.* I discuss the concept of the feminine mystique in further detail in Chapter 2.

11. For a discussion of androgyny in Lawrence, see Rachela Permenter's unpublished dissertation (223-37, 335-92). In this study Permenter concludes that though Lawrence reaches for nonduality, he remains limited by his "human separateness" (391).

12. I discuss Lawrence's portrayal of androgyny in detail in Chapter 4.

Chapter 2

13. For instance, stories such as "Daughters of the Vicar" and "Second Best" demonstrate how a female character moves toward marriage, while stories such as "Strike Pay" and "The White Stocking" demonstrate how the female character comes to terms with the marriage relation. Other stories work a variation upon these themes. In several, a female character, who appears to be exercising her choice and fighting to retain her independence, undergoes a change of heart at the very last moment—a theme found in "The Horse Dealer's Daughter," "Mother and Daughter," and "The Princess." Finally, some stories such as "Wintry Peacock" and "Fanny and Annie" suggest an untold story of the unmarried female character. Lawrence's marginalization of this character becomes apparent when we see that she is faintly sketched in contrast to the female character who is (or becomes) the male character's wife.

14. See John Worthen for a further discussion of Lawrence's use of autobiography to come to terms with his life (148-50).

15. Harris explains that the three versions of this story from "Intimacy" (1911) to "The White Woman" (1913) to the posthumously published version

"The Witch a la Mode" (1934) are basically the same in content (264-65 n34 and 37).

16. Mary Daly discusses the etymological associations of the word "witch" in Norwegian and Icelandic culture with the concept of aversion, whereas in more modern times this word has come to be associated with attraction, especially feminine seductiveness (*Pure Lust* 387-88).

17. Black uses Lawrencean biography to interpret this story. He reads Winifred and Coutts' conflict in terms of Lawrence's unresolved relations with his mother and girlfriends, Jessie Chambers and Helen Corke. (For further biographical readings of this story also see Tedlock 19-21; Delavenay 72, 104; Worthen 311-14.) Black also compares this story to some of Lawrence's earlier works such as "A Modern Lover" and *The Trespasser*. He suggests that in all three works, the man wants the woman, "or thinks he does, but what she wants of him is a strange parasitic relationship which he finally identifies and rejects" (131).

18. Though both unmarried women and married women have been equated to witches in cultural and literary history, Lawrence's portrayal of Winifred—an unmarried woman—as a witch emphasizes the potential threat she would represent to Coutts within a marriage relation.

19. *Malleus Maleficarum* or *Hammer of Witches* (Trans. Montague Summers. London: The Pushkin Press, 1948 [1928]) is a fifteenth century treatise that served as a key text during the Inquisition. Penelope also refers to Carolyn Merchant's *The Death of Nature*, which discusses a relation between natural science and witch burnings. In *The Newly Born Woman*, Helene Cixous and Catherine Clement discuss Freud's parallel between the women in *Malleus Maleficarum* and his own patients, 10-14. Another useful book on this subject is *Root of Bitterness: Documents of the Social History of American Women.* Ed. Nancy F. Cott. This book traces the social history of American women from the seventeenth- to the twentieth century. Cott refers to Kai Erikson's *Wayward Puritans* (N. Y.: Wiley Press, 1966), a study of seventeenth century Puritan New England. This latter book sees a deviance in three episodes that involve women:

the Antinomian crisis, the Quaker women scare, and the Salem witch trials. *The Patriarch's Wife: Literary Evidence and the History of the Family* by Margaret J. M. Ezell discusses the twentieth century model of turning to the past for self-analysis. In doing so, Ezell uses the seventeenth century to find a model for existing domestic patriarchy. The chapter, "The Good Wife," 36-61, is especially useful in reconstructing seventeenth century notions of what a good wife should be like. *Language, Gender and Society* includes a series of essays edited by Barrie Thorne, Cheris Kramarae and Nancy Henley. These incorporate the new research in the field os socio- and psycho-linguistics in the arena of feminist studies. They emphasize the change in "relations between language structure and language use, the move from the study of isolated variables to the study of usage in social context, and reconceptualizations of sex and gender." They "argue that increased attention to woman-woman talk involves an important redirection of research on language and gender" (3). *The Subversion of Women as Practised by Churches, Witch-Hunters and other Sexists*, by Nancy Van Vuuren, discusses the treatment of women by various sexist groups. Van Vuuren also provides a detailed bibliography on this topic (187-89).

20. Daniel Albright, in *Personality and Impersonality,* discusses Lawrence's use of the Lady of Shallott image as an image of female malevolence. He claims that her emotional remoteness leaves her, finally, alone (32-40).

21. For further details, refer to *This Sex Which is Not One* by Luce Irigaray (22-33). See also, *Thinking Through the Body* by Jane Gallop (92-99).

22. Coutts' desire for Winifred to "give" more than she is willing to give is reminiscent of Cyril Mersham's admonishment to Muriel in "A Modern Lover," where he tells her to live—and not alone: "You must have a flint and a steel, both, to make the spark fly. Supposing you be my flint, to spurt out red fire for me . . . [because] thought . . . [is] not life" (9). Like Cyril, Coutts is waiting for Winifred to "give" him strength.

23. We are not told her age, but the story suggests that she is a little younger than her sisters, who are about thirty years of age.

24. Lawrence explores the theme of the inhibiting and emotionally stultifying effect of authority in several of his works. For example, both Mr. Bates in "Odour of Chrysanthemums" and Mr. Morel in *Sons and Lovers*, are alcoholics. While the wives take charge of the situation, the children learn to be quiet and repressed. But as the children grow older, they assert their separateness in independent acts. For instance, the latter Paul, in *Sons and Lovers*, and Ursula and Gudrun, in *Women in Love,* rebel against their father's "bullying." Even the Rockley women try to resist their father in "You Touched Me" (I discuss this story in detail in the course of this chapter).

See also Tedlock (29-30) and Delavenay (186-87) for a discussion of authority and its effect on the children in "The Christening."

25. Lawrence complicates the issue by presenting Laurie, the male child, as also under the father's dominating influence. But though Laurie remains outside the main action of the christening, he contributes to his sister's shame by mocking her and thus allying himself with the male order within the text.

See also Harris' brief note on the lack of a dominating maternal influence in this story (79).

26. Past studies such as Widmer's, Draper's, and Harris', as briefly discussed above, focus on the nature of authority and the theme of sexual politics or male domination and female submission in this story.

27. This evocation in turn echoes the patriarchal attitudes of the Ancients toward women. For example, especially during the Renaissance, carnality was associated with shame and death. Olga Lucia Valbuena, in "Sorcery, Love Magic, and the Inquisition of Linguistic Sorcery in Celestina," discusses the influence of *Malleus Maleficarum* or *Hammer of Witches*, a misogynist tract written in the fifteenth century, on the subversion of women during the Renaissance period. Heinrich Kramer and James Sprenger, the two authors of this text, claimed that carnality in women leads to the spiritual death of the man. They assert that "all witchcraft comes from carnal lust, which is in women insatiable," and that

> though the devil tempted Eve to sin, yet Eve seduced Adam. And as the sin of Eve would not have brought death to our soul and body unless the sin had afterwards passed on to Adam, to which he was tempted by Eve, not by the devil, therefore she is more bitter than death. (quoted in Valbuena 209)

Valbuena explains that *Malleus Maleficarum* associates witchcraft with carnality and associates them both with the Fall because "God allows more power of witchcraft over the genital functions, on account of the first corruption of sin which came to us from the act of generation" (quoted in Valbuena 209). "[I]nstead of viewing the serpent as the instigator of the sin" (209), Kramer and Sprenger even hold the woman responsible for corrupting the serpent. Valbuena proceeds to note that such notions as this German text propagates are common among "the Judaic and Christian tradition" (209). In fact, Kramer and Sprenger's misogynist ideas are derived from Hesiod's *Theogony* and Herodotus' *Histories*, "where the myth of echidna, a voracious female serpent . . . [,] anticipates the horror of the female body with its sexual reproductive power" (209). Valbuena agrees with John Bugge that for gnostic Christian thinkers, "just as sexual intercourse provides for the replenishment of physical life, it also insures the continuation of death" (quoted in Valbuena 209).

The church encouraged the connection between sexuality and sin in women. Nancy Van Vuuren discusses the intolerance displayed by the church toward a display of sexuality in women. She says that

> the church was not particularly tolerant of independent women and defined women by their sexuality, which was considered by nature sinful. The woman who was acceptable to the church was the repentant woman who spent her life cloistered or serving men in order to do penance for her original sin. (72)

Not only was any kind of carnality considered sinful, but having a child out of wedlock was considered shameful, and was even a punishable crime during earlier periods in history. Van Vuuren asserts that religious orthodoxy proscibed any attempt by unmarried women to move outside the bounds of acceptable social behavior. For example, she says that the *Bible* defines silence as the most appropriate behavior for women. "[L]et your women keep silence in the churches: for it is not permitted unto them to speak; but they are commanded to be under obedience, as also saith the law" (I *Corinthians* 14: 34-35, 40).

28. Lawrence focuses on the symbol of the child, especially in his early fiction such as *Sons and Lovers* and *The Rainbow.* His later works, perhaps influenced by his increasingly darkening vision of the world during the war period, focus largely on the male-female relation as terminal. Though he wrote "The Christening" in 1912, he was revising it even as late as 1914 (Sagar, *D.H. Lawrence: A Calendar of His Works* 29, 54). During this time he was also writing *The Rainbow*. His state of mind at the time becomes clear when we note that "retrospectively in a letter of July 1917 [he said] that 'in the world of Europe I see no rainbow . . . no Ararat will rise above the subsiding iron water'" (quoted in Ross 45). Despite this statement, Ross points out the seeds of regeneration in the relation between Birkin and Ursula at the end of *Women in Love*. My focus is different. Ursula loses her child at the end of *The Rainbow*, though she does see the rainbow at the end. After *The Rainbow*, Lawrence's works focus on just the male-female relation.

29. See John Russell's article on Lawrence's association with painting ("D. H. Lawrence and Painting" 234-43).

30. Lawrence wrote this story a month after he wrote "Monkey Nuts."

31. Penelope, in *Speaking Freely*, discusses how the terms "old maid" and "spinster" "are often used as euphemisms . . . to emphasize the cultural assumption that a woman's only social identity is defined in terms of men and to avoid saying Lesbian" (105).

32. Refer to section I on "The Witch a la Mode" in this chapter for a further explanation of Lawrence's ideas on sharing a kiss on the mouth.

33. Refer to Widmer (58-59) and Harris (151-52, 258 n14, 282 n12-13).

34. For a reading of this story as a parallel to Lawrence's *The Fox*, refer to Tedlock (114) and Harris (150-51).

35. See my discussion of Lawrence's ideas on a mouth-kiss when shared by lovers in the section on "The Witch a la Mode."

36. Later in this chapter I shall discuss "Two Blue Birds" where Mrs. Gee, having established her independence from her husband, does not like to be kissed by him. She is outspoken and sexually liberated.

37. For a reading of this story in terms of Lawrencean biography, refer to Widmer (56).

38. I discuss "The Overtone" more completely in Chapter 3. Refer to Harris for biographical references in this story (175-76).

39. Lawrence believed that the "War finished . . . [him]: it was the spear through the side of all sorrows and hopes" (*Collected Letters* I 309). I discuss the significance of "The Risen Lord" in my section on *The Escaped Cock* in Chapter 4.

40. In the next sentence, however, the narrator says that James allows the policeman "to support her" (634). But the content of the text suggests that though James may allow the policeman to physically support her, she does not accept anything beyond his arm. The policeman's insignificance to James is especially apparent when she tells Marchbanks that he was "only incidental" (644).

41. Lawrence did not consider martyrdom and sacrifice very highly. He believed that sacrifice was a consequence of too much giving, and indicated imbalance in a relationship. Though this association suggests his disapproval of Marchbanks, he still presents Marchbanks' relations as more positive than those of James.

42. For a biographical reading of this story, refer to Harris (208).

43. Rich refers to "Michelle Cliff's 'Notes on Speechlessness' in *Spinster Wisdom* no. 5 [that] led Catherine Nicolson (in the same issue) to write of the power of 'deafness,' the frustration of our speech by those who do not want to hear what we have to say" (186).

44. See my earlier reference to Lawrence's views on kissing in the section on "The Witch a la Mode."

45. Refer to endnote 13.

46. Interestingly, Lawrence adopts the metaphor of the wolf for Marchbanks in "The Last Laugh" to emphasize his "natural" place in a traditionally ordered world where the man is the predator and the woman is the seductress.

47. Penelope, in *Speaking Freely*, discusses the often pejorative use of the term "girl." She explains that by contrasting "girl" with "man," women are equated with children while men are cast as adults. The term "girl" is also used as a euphemism for a lesbian (104-05). Mrs. Gee's use of the term "girl" for Miss Wrexall therefore implies an insult to the secretary.

Chapter 3

48. "The Thorn in the Flesh," written in 1913, may also be read as an example of a story about a young unmarried female from the serving class. This story situates Emilie in the same line of young female protagonists as the prostitutes in "The Primrose Path" and the tram conductors in "Tickets, Please." Like them, Emilie, too, is sexually liberated. But unlike the other females' experiences, Emilie's initiation is couched in Christian terms (as is Yvette's initiation in *The Virgin and the Gipsy*). The Christian overtones may result from the fact that both these experiences are first experiences. "The Thorn in the Flesh" initially focuses on Bachmann's dilemma (his fatal blow to his officer), and later on the consummation of his passion for Emilie. While we are informed of Emilie's attraction to him, she never actively pursues this interest.

Circumstantial need (Bachmann's need to flee the country to escape arrest and his need to forget his fear for his life) acts as the catalyst to their consummation. Though Lawrence uses religious metaphors to portray the rightness of their passion, Emilie remains a silent and incidental presence in the background. Since I have included a detailed study of "The Primrose Path," also written in 1913 and representative of the lower-class, economically impoverished but sexually liberated, young unmarried female, I do not discuss "The Thorn in the Flesh" in further detail in this chapter.

Initially, "The Princess" focuses on the impact of Colin Urquart's love for his daughter, Dolly, whom he affectionately calls his princess. After his death, at the age of thirty-eight, his virgin daughter travels with her female companion to Mexico, where she is attracted to the young and impoverished Romero. Alone in the mountains, they consummate their passion, but later she changes her decision and refuses to marry him. Because she is forced to stay with him in the mountains and to physically submit to him, she finally fatally shoots him. This experience turns her old and mad. The final line of the story, however, abruptly informs us that she later marries and is now "pleased."

"Mother and Daughter" dramatizes a confrontational relationship between Rachel Bodoin and her daughter, Virginia. After Rachel breaks up Virginia's relationship with Henry, she infects Virginia with her own evil humor so that Virginia too begins to put men down. While Virginia, like Dolly, has an independent income, she also works at a clerical job. Her mother, however, wishes her to discontinue this job, for she feels that it is turning her into an "old maid." They live together for five years when finally Virginia, now over thirty, agrees to marry an ugly, old Armenian who is over sixty and is on the lookout for a woman with a dowry.

49. I have included a brief discussion of this story in this section because, here, Lawrence discusses his ideas about Pan, Christ, and Isis in Search. These three mythic characters form a crucial part of his fictional vision.

50. See my discussion of "The Christening" in Chapter 2.

51. For a more detailed explanation of the treatment of women as witches, see my discussion of "The Witch a la Mode" in Chapter 2.

52. Catherine Mackinnon, in "Pornography: On Morality and Politics," defines pornography as "an industry that mass produces sexual intrusion on, access to, possession and use of women by and for men for profit. It exploits women's sexual and economic inequality for gain. It sells women to men as and for sex" (195).

Elizabeth Fox-Genovese, in *Feminism Without Illusions*, further expands on Mackinnon's and other feminists' views about pornography in our culture. She asserts that not only does pornography objectify women to men's sexual gaze but also to their power (87-111).

Judith Walkowitz finds the radical feminist attacks on commercial sex to be old fashioned. She traces such attacks to early feminist campaigns against male vice and the double standard, and associates them with the movement against pornography (1-9).

53. For a history of the rise of prostitution and flash houses, refer to *A History of Criminal Law and its Administration from 1750.* Here, Leon Radzinowicz discusses the implications of secular and religious administration on this phenomenon (287-306).

54. Though both Widmer and Harris discuss the pagan quality of this story, by making a more specific reference to two Dionysian myths where Dionysius is "torn to pieces" (137), Harris shows that the whole episode assumes connotations of mythic destruction. Harris also points out Lawrence's similar use of imagery in *The Rainbow* (1913-14) to describe the Ursula-Skrebensky relation. Here, she traces the parallels between Skrebensky's and John Raynor's attitude toward the women with whom they go out.

Harris also refuses to read this story as an illustration of "a war-torn society in which the women have taken the upper hand to the detriment of themselves and the men" (139).

55. Betty Friedan, in *The Feminine Mystique*, elaborates on how women's history is shrouded in the cult of wife and motherhood. David Bouchier, in *The Feminist Challenge*, discusses the contribution and impact of Friedan's polemic on the women's movement (42-44).

56. Delavenay, in *D. H. Lawrence: The Man and His Work*, discusses the first version of this tale where Annie's decision is final, but in the later version Lawrence casts doubt on its finality (437).

57. Miss Stokes' initials, M. S., evoke many women's decision to be referred to as "Ms." The initials "Ms." for a woman denote her decision not to be identified as either a "Miss"—an unmarried woman, or a "Mrs."—a married woman. Linguists, however, point out that the term "Ms." for women does not function in society in the same way as does the term "Mr." for men. For many women and men "Ms." is a term appropriated by those unmarried women who wish to disguise the fact that they are not married.

58. Lawrence's use of animal imagery to delineate character is apparent in several of his works such as *The Fox*, where Grenfel is associated with the hunting instincts of the fox. In *The Escaped Cock* Lawrence draws upon the restiveness of the rooster as well as plays on the word cock as a slang for the penis to emphasize the life of the flesh in the resurrected Christ (I develop this point in my next chapter on the short novels).

59. I discuss the theme of Isis in Search in relation to *The Escaped Cock* in Chapter 4. In this short novel, though Lawrence ends by depicting the union between the risen man and the woman of Isis, he also depicts the transformation of Madeleine from a whore to a madonna and the risen man's transformation from Christ to Pan.

Chapter 4

60. See E. W. Tedlock, Harry T. Moore, and R. P. Draper.

61. Unlike my separate discussions of the older and younger unmarried female characters in the short stories, I do not discuss them separately in relation to the short novels.

I do not discuss *The Captain's Doll* in this chapter. For though this tale refers to unmarried female characters, these references are brief. Further,

Lawrence's treatment of Hannele is similar to his treatment of March in *The Fox* that was written about the same time. Briefly, *The Captain's Doll*, written in 1921, revolves around the extra-marital relation of Captain Hepburn with Hannele. But after his wife dies under mysterious circumstances (the Captain is in the next room when his wife falls out of a window), the Captain turns away from Hannele because he is now attracted to very young girls, and wishes that he could marry a couple of them. He is flattered by the way they look up to him, and think he's "something wonderful" (92). Soon, however, he turns back to Hannele. Though Hannele initially resists him, she finally submits.

The unmarried female characters in this tale are Mitchka, Hannele's friend, and the young girls of seventeen and eighteen to whom the Captain feels attracted after his wife's death. In the story, Mitchka is soon dismissed from the action when she dies in an accident. The other set of unmarried female characters figure in the main action only as objects of the Captain's thoughts. Consequently, we only have a thumb-nail sketch of them. The action suggests that the Captain is attracted to these young women because of their silence which denies them any existence.

62. Albert J. Devlin, in "The 'strange and fiery' Course of *The Fox*: D. H. Lawrence's Aesthetic of Composition and Revision," discusses the nature of difference of the two endings. While the first version ends with March's acceptance of Grenfel's proposal and Banford's attendant dismay, the second version delineates more clearly the tension among Banford, March, and Grenfel. It also ends violently in Banford's murder (75-91). Also see "The Continuity of Lawrence's Short Novels" by Monroe Engel for a discussion on the weakness of the ending (*D. H. Lawrence: A Collection of Critical Essays.* Ed. Mark Spilka, 93-95). Further, Julian Moynahan, in "Lawrence, Woman, and the Celtic Fringe," traces the treatment of celtic themes in his discussion of the ending (*Lawrence and Women.* Ed. Anne Smith, 129-30).

63. In certain cultures, especially the Islamic culture, different types of veils are used to cover various parts of the body. For example, the *burkha* is a garment that covers the woman's body from head to toe. Made of various types of materials (depending on the wealth of the individual), it has holes or slits to aid sight, and a face piece that can be lifted for the purpose of eating. The *chadder* is

a heavy winding sheet that women are required to wear over their clothes. It must conceal them entirely, leaving only their faces open to the public. The *yashmak* is a small veil that covers the mouth.

64. See Elaine Showalter's essay on "Critical Cross-dressing" for a discussion on the idea of cross-dressing among genders.

65. Monroe Engel discusses the gender implications of the Grenfel-fox association (93-94; also Becker 125-26). These critics focus on Grenfel's sexual domination over the two females. Further, Mark Spilka traces the history of the demise of the wilful characters in Lawrence's fiction as a result of wish-fulfillment (195-96). Finally, Claude Sinzelle argues for a similarity between March and Grenfel to assert their complicity in Banford's death (173-74).

66. In my view, a lesbian relation is marked by a sexual interest—expressed or unexpressed—between females. A female friendship, by contrast, is non-sexual in nature.

67. As with female homosexuality, I believe male homosexuality expresses a sexual interest—active or inactive—between men. But an inactive interest does not necessarily suggest the fulfillment of such desires because sometimes the inactive interest is confused, often by the person concerned, with his desire for friendship. Similarly, an expressed desire for bonding with the same sex may be misread as an inactive interest in homosexuality.

68. Roger Austen's *Playing the Game* posits homophobia as the cause for lack of interest in the homosexual in literature (xi). His book traces the treatment of the homosexual from a general overview of the nineteenth-century to post-1960. Dr. Hendrik M. Ruitenbeek, in *Homosexuality and Creative Genius*, discusses the association between homosexuality and creativity. He accepts Freud's contribution to liberating homosexuality from the realm of "psychopathology into the area of neurosis" (xi), but also emphasizes the new shift to neo-Freudian and existentialist criticism. Today, homosexuality is associated with the question of identity as well as with the problems of sexual expression. Ruitenbeek quotes both Freud and such other ego psychologists as

Ernest Kris to show the link between artistic creativity and "some repressed libidinal or aggressive impulse" (xiv). Jeffrey Meyers, in *Homosexuality and Literature*, also traces the connection between homosexuality and creativity. See pp. 131-61 for a discussion on D. H. Lawrence. Georges-Michel Sarotte discusses male homosexuality in the American novel and theater in *Like a Brother, Like a Lover*. Part I is especially useful in tracing the evolution of the American "establishment" and its manifestation in literature (3-33). In response to the treatment of women in history, Adrienne Rich, in *On Lies, Secrets, and Silence*, discusses the need for a radical feminism—a movement that is entirely woman centered (223-30). Jane Rule, in *Lesbian Images,* studies the images of lesbians in literature. Her background study of the treatment of lesbians in history is especially illuminating (12-49).

69. Pamela Sargent, in her introduction to *The New Women of Wonder*, discusses the changing trends in the presentation of sexuality in science fiction. She discusses how in Samuel Delany's *Triton* (1976) individuals are presented without a fixed gender or sexual code (xvii).

70. In 1924, in a letter to Curtis Brown, Lawrence said that this tale can be called "Two Ladies and a Horse" (quoted in Sagar, *D. H. Lawrence: Life into Art* 139). This second title especially focuses on the relationship of Lou and her mother, Mrs. Witt, with their horse, *St. Mawr.*

71. In the beginning, we are briefly told that the unmarried Lou has an affair with Rico and quickly marries him, only to get bored with him just as quickly.

Refer to Harris for an overview of the critical debate surrounding this tale. Harris especially emphasizes her own presentation of Lawrence's ambivalenceand feminism in contrast to Julian Moynahan's judgement of the tale as "the stoutest blow Lawrence ever struck for women's liberation" (291 n4).

72. Refer to my discussion in Chapter 1 of Lawrence's ideas on cocksure women.

73. There is no definite portrayal of the other Manby sister in this tale.

74. James Wyly, in *The Phallic Quest: Priapus and Masculine Inflation*, discusses how Priapus, a Greek god famous for the enormous size of his genitals, is often seen as a metaphor for modern-day patriarchy and its search for power.

75. Keith Sagar discusses, eshaustively, the significance of horses in Lawrence's life and art (*D. H. Lawrence: Life into Art* 246-77).

76. Refer to my discussion of "Two Blue Birds" in Chapter 2 for a feminist reaction such as that of Adrienne Rich to metaphors of predatoriness when used by men for women.

77. I shall discuss this point in greater detail in my next section on *The Escaped Cock*.

78. Since very little detail surrounds Lucille, Yvette's older sister, I do not discuss her in any detail in this chapter. In brief, she is the more level-headed of the two sisters. In comparison to Yvette, she even finds some secretarial work to do in the city. Yet Yvette sees the longing in her eyes to be with a man (528), a longing that contradicts her assertion of indifference about wanting to be married.

79. Also see Stella Georgoudi's "Creating a Myth of Matriarchy," for a critique of J. J. Bachofen's view of matriarchy (*A History of Women in the West* 449-63).

80. See John Humma's discussion of "Insides and Outsides" in *The Virgin and the Gipsy: Metaphor and Meaning in D. H. Lawrence's Later Novels* (77-84).

81. Significantly, Lawrence does not focus on Uncle Fred, a bachelor of forty, who just lives for himself (472) and whose life we may infer is considerably less oppressed than that of Aunt Cissie, his sister.

82. Refer to Sandra Gilbert and Susan Gubar's *The Madwoman in the Attic* for a discussion on madness and rage in nineteenth-century literature by women

(77-80, 85-89, 90-92, 483-84). Also refer to Nina Baym's essay, "The Madwoman and her Languages" (45-61).

83. In *Women in Love*, Gudrun is also referred to as a witch. Draper calls Yvette a "descendent of Gudrun" (142).

Turner traces the Lady of Shallott metaphor in Lawrence to his impatience with the nineteenth-century tradition "where the impingements of reality upon artistic and sexual fantasy were either dreaded as a kind of death or longed for as a *Liebstod*" (154).

84. Lawrence's disillusionment with society, especially due to his war-time experiences, and his desire to escape from England to America (where he hoped to find a greater freedom) are well-documented (*Collected Letters* I 311, 353).

85. Janice Harris discusses briefly, but succinctly, the critical debate surrounding this novella as a "vision of resurrection and relationship" (302-05 n55-61). See also James C. Cowan's account of this relation in *D. H. Lawrence and the Trembling Balance* (237-54).

86. At the time of its first publication, the original title, *The Escaped Cock*, was considered too scandalous. It was therefore suggested that the more innocous title, *The Man Who Died,* be used. While Lawrence was adamantly opposed to this, he was unable to have his way.

87. Lawrence also associates Christ's sacrifice with the promise of power in "The Witch a la Mode." See my discussion of this story in Chapter 2.

88. Janice Harris asserts that Brewster's memory of the tale's inception is incorrect (302 n54).

89. Keith Sagar traces the genesis of *The Escaped Cock* to Lawrence's life-long desire for a life of community (*D.H. Lawrence: Life into Art* 278-323).

90. See Widmer for a biographical parallel between the risen man and a disillusioned Lawrence (207-08).

91. Both Harris and Hough discuss the need to read this tale in the context of the history of the Christian civilization, a history that Lawrence often contests. Hough, in "Lawrence's quarrel with Christianity: *The Man Who Died*," discusses Lawrence's long dispute with Christianity. "For Christianity, as Lawrence always sees it, is the attempt to live from the love-motive alone—to make love, *caritas*, pure altruism the only motive in life," says Hough (102). Hough claims that Lawrence disregards or misunderstands the evolutionary nature of Christianity (103).

92. See Lewiecki-Wilson for a discussion of *The Escaped Cock* as a re-enactment of the Oedipus complex (186-205).

Chapter 5

93. Lawrence's advocacy of sexual liberation among women may also be contradictory and ineffective because of his belief in woman's "natural" (essentialist) yearning for the male. In other words, his struggle between feminist concerns and the patriarchy is most evident in the short fiction where he depicts more assertive women.

94. Refer to endnote 20.

95. Though Lawrence's comparison of Winifred with a witch is more apparent because of the story's title, his similar comparison of Miss James is apparent in the textual action.

96. Feminists especially validate mother-daughter relations among women as a means of stregthening their female lineage, and countering the impact of the patriarchy.

97. Commenting on his belief in the heterosexual, Lawrence had said:

> You've got to marry the pair of them. Apart, they're no good. The emotions that have not the approval and inspiration of the mind are just

hysterics. The mind without the approval and inspiration of the emotions is just a dry stick, a dead tree, no good for anything. ("On Human Destiny" 625)

Works Cited

Works by D.H.Lawrence

Lawrence, D.H. "Cocksure Women and Hensure Men," in *Phoenix II: Uncollected, Unpublished, and Other Prose Works by D. H. Lawrence*. Ed. Warren Roberts and Harry T. Moore. New York: Viking, 1968 (1959). 553-555.

———. "Do Women Change?" in *Phoenix II*. 539-542.

———. *Fantasia of the Unconscious*. London: Heinneman, 1935.

———. "Give Her a Pattern" in *Phoenix II*. 535-38.

———. *Lady Chatterley's Lover*. Middlesex, England: Penguin, 1979 (1928).

———. "Master in His Own House," in *Phoenix II*. 546-48.

———. "Matriarchy," in *Phoenix II*. 549-552.

———. "On Being a Man," in *Phoenix II*. 616-22.

———. “On Human Destiny,” in *Phoenix II*. 623-29.

———. *Sons and Lovers*. Cambridge: Cambridge UP, 1992.

———. *The Collected Letters Of D. H. Lawrence*. Ed. Harry T. Moore. Vol. I. London: Heinemann, 1962.

———. *The Collected Letters of D.H. Lawrence*. Ed. Harry T. Moore. Vol. II. London: Heinemann, 1962.

———. *The Complete Short Novels.* Middlesex, England: Penguin, 1982. (I shall refer to each short novel by its title and its page number in this complete edition).

———. *The Complete Short Stories*. Vol. I. London: Penguin, 1976. 1-282.

———. *The Complete Short Stories*. Vol. II. London: Penguin, 1976. 283-586.

———. *The Complete Short Stories*. Vol. III. London: Penguin, 1977. 587-853. (The three volumes of *The Complete Short Stories* follow consecutive page numbering; the story and page number placed within the text.)

———. *The Lost Girl.* Cambridge: Cambridge UP, 1979.

———. *The Rainbow*. Cambridge: Cambridge UP, 1989.

———. “The Risen Lord,” in *Phoenix II*. 571-77.

———. *Women in Love*. New York: Penguin, 1989.

Other Works

Acworth, Evelyn. *The New Matriarchy*. London: Victor Gollancz, 1965.

Albright, Daniel. *Personality and Impersonality: Lawrence, Woolf, and Mann*. Chicago: U of Chicago P, 1978.

Andriano, Joseph. *Our Ladies Of Darkness: Feminine Daemonology in Male Gothic Fiction*. University Park: Pennsylvania State UP, 1993.

Ardener, Shirley. "The Representation of Women in Academic Models." *Visibility and Power: Essays on Women in Society and Development.* Ed. Leela Dube, Eleanor Leacock, and Shirley Ardener. Delhi: Oxford UP, 1986. 3-14.

Austen, Roger. *Playing the Game. The Homosexual Novel in America*. New York: Bobbs-Merrill, 1977.

Baker, J. H. *An Introduction to English Legal History*. London: Butterworths, 1990.

Baym, Nina. "The Madwoman And Her Languages: Why I Don't Do Feminist Theory." *Feminist Issues in Literary Scholarship*. Ed. Shari Benstock. Indianapolis: Indiana UP, 1987. 45-61.

Beauvoir, Simone de. *The Second Sex*. Trans. and Ed. H. M. Parshley. New York: Knopf, 1952.

Becker, George J. *D. H. Lawrence*. New York: Ungar, 1980.

Belsey, Catherine, and Jane Moore. Introduction. *The Feminist Reader: Essays in Gender and the Politics of Literary Criticism*. Ed. Catherine Belsey and Jane Moore. Cambridge: Blackwell, 1991 (1989). 1-20.

Black, Michael. *D.H.Lawrence: The Early Fiction, A Commentary*. Cambridge, London: Cambridge UP, 1986.

Boone, Joseph Allen. *Engendering Men: The Question of Male Feminist Criticism*. New York: Routledge, 1990.

Bornstein, Diane. *The Lady in the Tower: Medieval Courtesy Literature for Women*. Hamden: Archon, 1983.

Bouchier, David. *The Feminist Challenge: The Movement for Women's Liberation in Britain and the USA.*. New York: Schocken, 1984.

Brandwein, Ruth A. "Toward Androgyny in Community and Organizational Practice." *Women, Power, And Change*. Eds. Ann Weick and Susan T. Vandiver. Washington, D.C.: National Association of Social Workers, 1982. 158-70.

Brownmiller, Susan. *Against our Will: Men, Women, and Rape*. New.York: Simon & Schuster, 1975.

Brumberg, Joan Jacobs. *Fasting Girls. The History of Anorexia Nervosa*. New York, Penguin, 1988.

Cadogan, Mary, and P. Craig. *Women and Children First: The Fiction of Two World Wars*. London: Gollancz, 1978.

Carr, Edward H. *What Is History?* New York: Knopf, 1963.

Cixous, Helene, and Catherine Clement. *The Newly Born Woman*. Trans. Betsy Wing. Minneapolis: U of Minnesota P, 1986.

Cowan, James C. *D. H. Lawrence and the Trembling Balance*. London: Penn State UP, 1990.

Daly, Mary. *Pure Lust: Elemental Feminist Philosophy*. Boston: Beacon Press, 1984.

Delavenay, Emile. *D. H. Lawrence: The Man and His Work, The Formative Years: 1885-1919*. Trans. Katherine Delavenay. London: Heinemann, 1972.

Devlin, Albert J. "The 'Strange and Fiery' Course of The Fox: D. H. Lawrence's Aesthetic of Composition and Revision." *The Spirit of D. H. Lawrence. Centenary Studies*. Eds. Gamini Salgado and G. K. Das. London: MacMillan Press, 1988. 75-91.

Diner, Helen. *Mothers and Amazons: The First Feminine History of Culture*. Trans. and Ed. John Philip Lundin. New York: Doubleday, 1973.

Dix, Carol. *D. H. Lawrence and Women*. London: MacMillan, 1980.

Doan, Laura L. Introduction. *Old Maids To Radical Spinsters: Unmarried Women in the Twentieth-Century Novel*. Ed. Laura L. Doan. Chicago: U of Illinois P, 1991. 1-16.

Draper, R. P. *D. H. Lawrence*. New York: Twayne, 1964.

Dworkin, Andrea. *Pornography: Men Possessing Women*. New York: Dutton, 1989.

Engel, Monroe. "The Continuity of Lawrence's Short Novels." *D. H. Lawrence: A Collection of Critical Essays*. Ed. Mark Spilka. Englewood Cliffs: Prentice-Hall, 1963. 93-100.

Ezell, Margaret. *The Patriarch's Wife: Literary Evidence and the History of the Family*. Chapel Hill: U of North Carolina P, 1987.

Ford, George H. *Double Measure: A Study of the Novels and Stories of D. H. Lawrence*. New York: Holt, 1965.

Fox-Genovese, Elizabeth. *Feminism without Illusions: A Critique of Individualism*. Chapel Hill: U of North Carolina P, 1991.

Friedan, Betty. *The Feminine Mystique*. New York: Dell Publishing, 1963.

Gallop, Jane. *Thinking Through the Body*. New York: Columbia UP, 1988.

Garfinkel, Paul E., and David M. Garner. *Anorexia Nervosa. A Multidimensional Perspective*. New York: Brunner/Mazel, Inc., 1982.

Georgoudi, Stella. "Creating a Myth of Matriarchy." *A History Of Women In The West.* Vol. I. *From Ancient Goddesses to Christian Saints*. Trans. Arthur Goldhammer. Ed. Pauline Schmitt Pantel. Cambridge: Belknap Press of Harvard UP, 1992. 449-63.

Gilbert, Sandra, and Susan Gubar. *The Madwoman in the Attic: The Woman Writer And The Nineteenth-Century Literary Imagination.* London: Yale UP, 1984.

Gilbert, Sandra. "Life's Empty Pack: Notes Toward a Literary Daughteronomy." *Literary Inquiry*. March 1985. 355-84.

Hall, Nor. *The Moon and the Virgin*. New York: Harper and Row, 1980.

Hardy, Barbara. "Women in D. H. Lawrence's Works." *D. H. Lawrence: Novelist, Poet, Prophet*. Ed. Stephen Spender. New York: Harper and Row, 1973.

Harris, Janice H. *The Short Fiction of D.H.Lawrence*. New Brunswick: Rutgers UP, 1984.

Heilbrun, Carolyn G. *Toward a Recognition Of Androgyny*. New York: Knopf, 1973.

Hill, Allette Olin. *Mother Tongue, Father Time: A Decade of Linguistic Revolt*. Bloomington: Indiana UP, 1986.

Holbrook, David. *Where D. H. Lawrence Was Wrong About Woman.* London: Associated UP, 1992.

Horn, Pierre L., and Mary Beth Pringle. *The Image of the Prostitute in Modern Literature*. New York: Ungar, 1984.

Hough, Graham. "Lawrence's Quarrel with Christianity: *The Man Who Died.*" *D. H. Lawrence: A Collection of Critical Essays*. Ed. Mark Spilka. Englewood Cliffs: Prentice-Hall, 1963. 101-11.

———. *The Dark Sun. A Study of D. H. Lawrence*. New York: Capricorn, 1956.

Humma, John B. *Metaphor And Meaning In D. H. Lawrence's Later Novels*. London: U of Missouri P, 1990.

Irigaray, Luce. *Speculum of the Other Woman*. Trans. Gillian C. Gill. New York: Cornell UP, 1985.

———. *This Sex Which Is Not One*. Trans. Catherine Porter and Carolyn Burke. New York: Cornell UP, 1985.

Kanowitz, Leo. *Women and the Law: The Unfinished Revolution.* Albuquerque: U of New Mexico P, 1969.

Kaplan, Alexandra, and Joan Bean. *Beyond Sex-Role Stereotypes: Readings Toward a Psychology of Androgyny*. Boston: Little, Brown, 1976.

Kiberd, Declan. *Men and Feminism in Modern Literature*. Hong Kong: MacMillan, 1985.

Kramarae, Cheris. *Women and Men Speaking. Frameworks for Analysis*. London: Newbury House, 1981.

Kramer, Heinrich, and James Sprenger. *Malleus Maleficarum*. Trans. Montague Summers. London: Pushkin, 1948 (1928).

Kristeva, Julia. *Desire in Language: A Semiotic Approach to Literature and Art.* New York:Columbia UP, 1980.

Lakoff, Robin. *Language and Woman's Place*. New York: Harper and Row, 1975.

Lewiecki-Wilson, Cynthia. *Writing Against the Family: Gender in Lawrence and Joyce*. Carbondale: Southern Illinois UP, 1994.

Mackinnon, Catherine. "Pornography: On Morality and Politics," in *Toward a Feminist Theory of the State*. Cambridge: Harvard UP, 1989.

Meyers, Jeffrey. H*omosexuality and Literature: 1890-1930*. Montreal: McGill-Queen's UP, 1977.

———. "D. H. Lawrence and Homosexuality." *D. H. Lawrence: Novelist, Poet, Prophet.* Ed. Stephen Spender. New York: Harper and Row, 1973. 135-46.

Miles, Margaret R. "The Virgin's One Bare Breast: Female Nudity and Religious Meaning in Tuscan Early Renaissance Culture." *The Female Body In Western Culture: Contemporary Perspectives*. Ed. Susan Rubin Suleiman. Cambridge: Harvard UP, 1986. 193-208.

Millett, Kate. *Sexual Politics*. New York: Avon, 1970.

Moi, Toril. *Sexual/Textual Politics: Feminist Literary Theory*. London: Methuen, 1985.

Moore, Burness E. "Psychoanalytic Meaning and Treatment of Frigidity." *Sexual Function and Dysfunction*. Ed. Paul J. Fink and Van Buren O. Hammett. Philadelphia: Davis, 1969. 67-84.

Moore, Harry T. *The Priest of Love: A Life of D.H.Lawrence*. New York: Farrar, Straus and Giroux, 1974 (1954).

Moynahan, Julian. "Lawrence, Woman, and the Celtic Fringe." *Lawrence and Women*. Ed. Anne Smith. London: Vision, 1978. 122-35.

Munich, Adrienne. "Notorious Signs, Feminist Criticism and Literary Tradition." *Making a Difference: Feminist Literary Criticism*. Ed. Gayle Greene and Coppelia Kahn. London: Routledge, 1985. 238-59.

Murry, John Middleton. *Son of Woman*. New York: Jonathan Cape and Harrison Smith, 1931.

Olsen, Tillie. *Silences*. New York: Delacorte Press, 1978.

Penelope, Julia. *Speaking Freely: Unlearning the Lies of the Fathers' Tongues*. New York: Pergamon, 1990.

Permenter, Rachela. "Nonduality: Romantic Postmodernism and Feminism in the Works of Herman Melville and D. H. Lawrence." Dissertation. Northern Illinois University, 1992.

Rabinowitz, Peter J. "Assertions and Assumptions: Fictional Patterns and the External World." in *PMLA*. 96.3 (May 1981): 408-19.

Radzinowicz, Leon. *A History of English Law and its Administration from 1750: The Clash Between Private Initiative And Public Interest In The Enforcement Of The Law*. Vol. II. London: Stevens and Sons, 1956.

Rich, Adrienne. *On Lies, Secrets, and Silence: Selected Prose. 1966-1978*. New York: Norton, 1979.

Riemer, James D. "Homosexuality in Science Fiction and Fantasy." *EroticUniverse: Sexuality and Fantastic Literature*. Ed. Donald Palumbo. New York: Greenwood, 1986. 145-61.

Root of Bitterness: Documents of the Social History of American Women. Ed. Nancy F. Cott. New York: Dutton, 1972.

Ross, Charles L. Introduction. *Women in Love*. London: Penguin, 1989.

Rossman, Charles. "'You are the call and I am the answer': *D. H. Lawrence and Women*," in *D. H. Lawrence Review*. 8.3 (Fall 1975): 255-328.

Ruitenbeek, Hendrik M. *Homosexuality and Creative Genius*. New York: Astor-Honor, 1967.

Rule, Jane. *Lesbian Images*. New York: Doubleday, 1975.

Russell, John. "D. H. Lawrence and Painting." *D. H. Lawrence: Novelist, Poet, Prophet*. Ed. Stephen Spender. New York: Harper and Row, 1973.

Sagar, Keith. *D, H. Lawrence: Life Into Art*. New York: Viking Penguin, 1985.

———. *D. H. Lawrence: A Calendar of his works*. Manchester: Manchester, UP, 1979.

Sargent, Pamela. Introduction. *The New Women of Wonder: Recent Science Fiction Stories By Women About Women*. Ed. Pamela Sargent.
New York: Vintage, 1978. xiii-xxxiv.

Sarotte, Georges-Michel. *Like a Brother, Like a Love*r. Trans. Richard Miller. New York: Doubleday, 1978.

Showalter, Elaine. Introduction. *Speaking of Gender*. Ed. Elaine Showalter. New York, London: Routledge, 1989. 1-13.

———. Ed. *The New Feminist Criticism: Essays on Women, Literature, and Theory*. New York: Pantheon, 1985.

———. "Critical Cross-Dressing: Male Feminists and the Woman of the Year," in *Raritan* (1983): 116-33.

Sinzelle, Claude. "Skinning the Fox: A Masochist's Delight." *D. H. Lawrence in the Modern World*. Eds. Peter Preston and Peter Hoare. London: MacMillan, 1989. 161-79.

Spilka, Mark. Ed. *D. H. Lawrence: A Collection of Critical Essays*. Englewood Cliffs: Prentice-Hall, 1963.

Spender, Dale. *Women of Ideas and what Men have done to them: From Aphra Behn to Adrienne Rich*. London: Ark, 1983.

Storch, Margaret. *Sons and Adversaries: Women in William Blake and D. H. Lawrence*. Knoxville: U of Tennessee P, 1990.

Tedlock, E.W., Jr. *D. H. Lawrence: Artist & Rebel. A Study of Lawrence's Fiction*. Albuquerque: U of New Mexico P, 1963.

Thorne, Barrie, Cheris Kramarae and Nancy Henley, Eds. *Language, Gender and Society*. London: Newbury, 1983.

Tual, Anny. "Speech and Silence: Women in Iran." *Visibility and Power: Essays on Women in Society and Development*. Eds. Leela Dube, Eleanor Leacock, and Shirley Ardener. Delhi: Oxford UP, 1986. 54-69.

Turner, John. "Purity and Danger in D. H. Lawrence's *The Virgin and the Gipsy*." *D. H. Lawrence: Centenary Essays*. Ed. Mara Kalnins. Bristol: Bristol Classical, 1986.

Valbuena, Olga Lucia. "Sorceresses, Love Magic, and the Inquisition of Linguistic Sorcery in Celestina" in *PMLA* 109.2 (March 1994): 207-224.

Van Vuuren, Nancy. *The Subversion Of Women As Practiced By Churches, Witch-Hunters, And Other Sexists*. Philadelphia: Westminster, 1938.

Von Beit, Hedwig. "Concerning The Problem Of Transformation In The Fairy Tale." *Perspectives in Literary Symbolism*. Vol. I. Ed. Joseph Strelka. London: Pennsylvania State UP, 1968. 48-71.

Walkowitz, Judith. *Prostitution and Victorian Society: Women, Class, and the State*. Cambridge: Cambridge UP, 1980.

Weil, Kari. *Androgyny and the Denial of Difference*. Charlottesville: UP of Virginia, 1992.

Wheeler, Richard. "Give and Take in 'Tickets, Please.'" in *The D. H. Lawrence Review* 10.3 (Fall 1977): 242-50.

Widmer, Kingsley. *The Art of Perversity: D. H. Lawrence's Shorter Fictions*. Seattle: U of Washington P, 1962.

Wittig, Monique. "The Mark of Gender." *The Poetics of Gender*. Ed. Nancy K. Miller. New York: Columbia UP, 1986. 63-73.

Women and Language in Transition. Ed. Joyce Penfield. New York: State U of New York P, 1987.

Woolf, Virginia. *A Room Of One's Own*. London: Harcourt Brace Jovanovich, 1981 (1929).

Worthen, John. *D. H. Lawrence: The Early Years, 1885-1912*. Cambridge: Cambridge UP, 1991.

Writing Differences. Readings from the seminar of Helene Cixous. Ed. Susan Sellers. New York: St. Martin's, 1988.

Wyly, James. *The Phallic Quest: Priapus and Masculine Inflation*. Toronto: Inner City, 1989.

Yaeger, Patricia, and Beth Kowaleski-Wallace. Introduction. *Refiguring the Father: New Feminist Readings of Patriarchy*. Carbondale: Southern Illinois UP, 1989.

Yaeger, Patricia. *Honey-Mad Women: Emancipatory Strategies in Women's Writing*. New York: Columbia UP, 1988.

Index